NO PATH TO ENLIGHTENMENT

The I before I am – *exposing the illusion of your Self*

NO PATH TO ENLIGHTENMENT

The I before I am – *exposing the illusion of your Self*

COLIN McMORRAN

COPYRIGHT

Copyright © 2022 by Colin McMorran.

All rights reserved. No part of this book may be reproduced, distributed or transmitted in any form by any means, electronic or mechanical, including photography, recording, or by any information storage and retrieval system without the prior written permission of the author, except for the inclusion of brief quotations in a review.

Design and typesetting by Simon Hawkesworth. Set in Dante and Bodoni Standard typefaces.

Cover image by Yasir Nadeem.

More information at:
seeingnow.com

CONTENTS

	Acknowledgements	11
	Preface	13
	Introduction	17
1	The Unknowable	21
2	The I before I am	25
3	My 'Story'	31
4	The Self	37
5	The Illusion	43
6	Spiritual Paths, Emptiness & Non-self	49
7	You are not what you think	61
8	Strategic Mind & Story Mind	71
9	Ego	77
10	Meet me there	83
11	Time	87
12	Inner Realms	95
13	Your Body	107
14	Consciousness	117
15	Indoctrination	127
16	Self Enquiry	135
17	Fate & Free Will	141
18	To Be and Not to Be	151
19	Setting Sail	157
20	Curtain Call	163
	Appendix	169
	Bibliography	175

Having a sweet taste of Enlightenment is not the same as being Enlightened, just as tasting the sweetness of honey is not the same as being honey – if it's sweetness you desire, realise that honey cannot taste itself.

COLIN McMORRAN

ACKNOWLEDGEMENTS

I would like to express my deepest gratitude to my partner Carolyn for her help and patience with the manuscript's early drafts and her unwavering belief in my writing and in me, her intuitive grasp of the narrative's underlying intent and her love and support have made this book possible. I would like to thank Mick for his friendship and his invaluable expertise; befriending a PhD scholar in ancient Hindu texts who is also a proof editor was synchronicity at its most bizarre. Huge thanks to Carl for countless correspondences and candid philosophical discussions over many years of friendship – *the first philosopher I found outside of a book*. I am grateful to Simon for his insightful feedback on the initial versions and to James for casting a trained eye over the science. Big thanks to Chris for his wonderful encouragement during the early drafts and to Angela for her heartfelt reflections and clarity of thought over the final versions. I would like to thank Lindsay for focusing her sparkling intellect over the whole writing style and for giving such an invaluable insight into the minds of my potential readers. I will be forever grateful to Julie for her passionate and intuitive feedback; her wholehearted support and friendship came at the perfect time. Lastly, thank you Si for your design and typesetting skills – your passion for books turned the manuscript into print.

PREFACE

In pursuit of knowledge, every day something is added. In the practice of the Tao, every day something is dropped.

TAO TE CHING

PREFACE

While from the perspective of the individual Self (you – the reader), this book might initially be seen to offer a nihilistic message – because it exposes the illusion of your Self, revealing nothing at your core, and therefore offering you nothing – it also bestows the potential to be liberated from the anxious, fearful and neurotic delusion that underpins the human condition. Therefore, rather than illuminating your search, I will try to consume it like a black hole drawing everything in and giving nothing back. Just as the unseen and immeasurable emptiness of space can only be comprehended indirectly through the objects existing within it, similarly the stillness underlying this message (and all phenomena) can only be pointed to indirectly through words. However, these words are not the stillness, just as objects are not the space they are held within. The stillness exists between the words and behind the concepts: it is what is absent, what is left unspoken. The illusionary Self is the 'knowing', the stillness is the 'unknowing' – the indefinable empty space without a position and without subject/object duality. The stillness is inherent in all things; it is what remains once the Self is stripped bare, it is where wisdom lives. If the illusionary Self is exposed leaving just the innate stillness it will be your greatest personal loss and yet the magnitude of the transformation will be incomprehensible, a paradox I will explore throughout the book.

The truth of this message does not require validation from a higher authority; do not look outside – validation lies within you. The stillness in which both clarity and confusion arise remains in a state of perfection

– untouched by your desire to know it, however, at a deeper level the illusionary Self may sense its own emptiness and be open to this message.

The illusionary Self believes it lives in a world of free will and choice and so at this precise moment what happens next appears to depend upon our individual choices: mine being the words I type, and yours being whether or not you choose to read them. The assumption that we have such a freedom of choice seems obvious but as I shall attempt to point out, that too is an illusion.

INTRODUCTION

We swallow greedily any lie that flatters us, but we sip only little by little at a truth we find bitter.

DENIS DIDEROT

INTRODUCTION

This book aims to liberate you from the illusionary Self and reveal that you are the stillness beneath – the one ocean that embraces all. If successful, you will no longer be a slave to your thoughts, in fact you will be open to see and hear for the first time; you will be free to experience the world as it is, as opposed to how it has been created through your conditioning and sustained by the illusion of your Self. This is, in the truest sense of the word, freedom. Freedom from your ingrained thought patterns, freedom from the defensive ego, freedom from the constraint of being what you think you should be, and freedom from anger, guilt, depression and sadness. You are not a separate person – the *I am*, you are the *I before I am* – the pure presence before separation. Another way of phrasing it is that you are not a separate person experiencing consciousness; you are consciousness experiencing a separate person.

I would like to make it clear from the outset that this book is not about positive thinking or about choosing positive thoughts over negative ones or about dropping thoughts. It is about recognising an underlying stillness that can notice thoughts rather than becoming them; it is about realising your true nature has little to do with your thoughts or the Self that is born from them. You are not the 'I am' born out of thought, you are the 'I' before thought – the *I before I am*. I will show that by noticing how the Self reacts to the world we can come to realise it is our attachment to thoughts – *not the thoughts themselves* – that creates the Self and leads to our suffering. Moreover, just as it is not about choosing positive thoughts over negative ones, neither is it about stopping or controlling your thoughts. It is quite obvious that we cannot stop the thoughts that wash over us, any more than we can stop the waves that break on the shore, however, we can look beneath those thoughts to the ocean they are held within. I will refer to this ocean of pure conscious awareness as the Absolute. *The I before I am* and *The Absolute* are different expressions used throughout the book for the same underlying truth.

I invite you to taste that truth. All that is required is an open mind and a willingness to enquire within. The illusion of the Self is the belief that you are your thoughts – in other words, the personal identification with the voice in your head (discussed further in Chapter 14), when in reality you are the awareness beneath that constant mind chatter. Noticing the thoughts rather than attaching to them may seem a subtle change in perspective, but in fact, it is a huge paradigm shift. Once you have taken a step back from your thoughts by not attaching to them, they become like clouds passing across a clear sky. You will notice the interesting patterns and shapes they form as they float by – coming from nothing and returning to nothing, but they cannot touch the background perfection of the azure blue stillness – the Absolute that holds all.

❄

In a sense, this message is unsettling because I am questioning the reality of that which wants to know – I am questioning *you*, which is not something many readers will welcome. To sense the ineffable ground of your being this message needs to resonate beyond who you believe you are. Nevertheless, it must first communicate on an intellectual level, before transcending both your Self and message.

You may be seeking answers, but if you assume this will be a journey of self-discovery, you should know that there is no journey being taken and no Self to discover. Consider this less of a personal journey and more an impersonal arrival. What follows is a flight of imagination within which I hope to expose the illusion of the individual Self – *the illusion of you*, and the futility of trying to add to or improve such an illusion. This discourse is open to anyone with an enquiring mind and I hope to expose the illusion of both the journey and the individual – *you*, who appears to be taking it. Once the illusion is exposed, all that remains is the stillness out of which all things arise. Trying to reveal you are that stillness – *the I before I am* – is at the heart of the book.

1

THE UNKNOWABLE

The eye does not go there, nor speech, nor mind. We do not know That. We do not know how to instruct one about it. It is distinct from the known and above the unknown.

KENA UPANISHAD

Not-Knowing is true knowledge. Presuming to know is disease. First realise that you are sick; then you can move towards health.

TAO TE CHING

THE UNKNOWABLE

How can the unknowable be approached, how can it be written or talked about? How can the infinite be expressed by the finite, how can the eternal and the formless be comprehended in a world of impermanence and forms? The unknowable stillness at the core of your being can only be pointed to indirectly and therefore I will approach the task from various angles.

In pragmatic terms, I will exert two fundamental issues: 1) that we are the unknowable Absolute – the impersonal 'I' that comes before the personal 'I am'; 2) that we have a delusional understanding of our relationship to the world around us, created by our thoughts. As mentioned, the first can only be pointed to indirectly. However, the second – *our delusional perspectives* – can be examined by focusing on our common assumptions about the world around us and how we interact with it, including our relationships with other people. In so doing we will explore common themes, such as time, space, free will, and consciousness, and show how these concepts create and sustain the illusion of a Self – of *your* Self. I will try to show how these beliefs are kept alive by our thinking, which builds and sustains our story – our self-image – a story that is unreal and, for the most part, unhelpful. I will offer a way to break the stranglehold of thought, expose the illusionary Self and bring you back to the present moment. In this way, you may begin to sense a deeper non-personal awareness – *the I before I am*.

This awareness can be glimpsed in those rare and uninvited moments of so-called 'heightened consciousness' or 'heightened awareness' that sometimes occur in a flash, but cannot be experienced or relived through memory. These moments may occur at times of great personal drama, physical exertion, quiet contemplation, or even while brushing your teeth – it matters not. The common factor is that for a fleeting instant and through no cultivated effort, an altered state takes over – a sort of peace and clarity that has nothing to do with our individual stories, and for a moment our suffering ends. In other words, because there is no personal 'I' having an 'experience', the moment cannot become part of our experiencing structure and we do not attach to it. Then we quickly return to everyday consciousness, wanting to understand and trying to take ownership of what we believed we just experienced – we want to make it part of our story. However, this impersonal awareness cannot be contextualised within our frame of reference; it can only live when we are absent.

This clarity exists all the time beneath the story of you. These brief glimpses cannot be expressed without destroying their essence, and so all I can do is to try to point to this *ground of being* indirectly through analogies and metaphors. It is not knowledge that can be understood and passed on; it is more akin to an ever-present and vaguely familiar feeling that infuses every experience, being both of the experience and *other than* the experience – both *real* and *unreal*. All that can be hoped for is that the Absolute lying behind everything, including the illusion of the Self, might become apparent *to no one*. By which I mean become apparent, not in a dualistic subject/object sense as in 'I am aware of this' or ' I know this', but in an impersonal, indescribable being-ness that is as fundamental and as effortless as breathing.

❈

The reasons people look beneath the surface appearance of life for meaning and purpose and seek spiritual paths or deep philosophical insights are many and varied. Perhaps you are looking for something to validate your experience of life and strengthen your worldview, or maybe you are interested in ideas that challenge that experience and the accompanying introspections and meditations. You may be confused and struggling to make sense of your life and perhaps suffering from depressive thoughts and feelings of hopelessness, you may be looking for a purpose – something that makes sense of the chaos that can pull you out of the darkness. You may have studied Eastern philosophy, have knowledge of non-duality, and may want to test a strong philosophical or spiritual conviction, or perhaps you have arrived with nothing more than an open mind and a passing interest. You may not consider yourself an overt seeker but may be open to new ways of looking at the world and your relationship to it.

Whatever your reasons, they will make little difference when it comes to comprehending this message because it is not about gaining and building upon existing concepts or comparing beliefs and faiths nor is it about replacing negative thoughts with positive ones. It is not a self-help book with positive affirmations designed to rescue you from mental anguish because there is no long-term benefit in adding to or building upon a Self that is illusionary – any positive gains would be short lived and you would soon return to suffering, searching and seeking. Nor is it about acquiring knowledge, therefore understanding Western philosophy, Eastern spirituality or religious scripture will be no more advantageous than knowledge of the periodic table or Greek alphabet – we are starting from a clean slate.

Regardless of the motives that brought you here, as you start to consider the implications of this message – *that who you believe you are is an illusion* – your initial response will likely be one of disbelief and incredulity. In fact, you will probably feel threatened and under attack. *'When someone beats a rug, the blows are not against the rug, but against the dust in it'* (Rumi). In order to continue, you will need to fight your knee-jerk reaction to the blows, which will not be easy because every fibre of your being will want to perpetuate your story. Just as the layers of dust built up over the years dull the brightness of the weave, so your conditioned mind builds up layers of identity obscuring the stillness beneath. This is not about revealing a truth; rather, it is about exposing the illusionary Self as a falsehood. If successful, there are no words for what happens thereafter.

2
THE I BEFORE I AM

The one you are looking for is the one who is looking.
ST FRANCIS OF ASSISI

Salvation is to see things as they already are.
NISARGADATTA MAHARAJ

In a sense, these words are coming from the 'I' before 'I am'. What do I mean by this? Well, they are coming from a deeper awareness, one that does not easily translate into the world of day-to-day thinking. They are coming from the ground of our being – a stillness underlying everything. However, within the world of the illusionary Self they have little authority or validity because that world deals in 'knowing' – this comes from unknowing.

This unknowing stillness has many names: The Buddha called it the empty mind, Jesus called it the Kingdom of Heaven, Eckhart Tolle calls it the light of consciousness or presence, Hindus call it the higher-self or Brahman, Rumi wrote *I know not myself* and the ancient Chinese called it the Tao or the Way. The Tao Te Ching begins with *the Tao that can be named is not the true Tao*. It is for this reason the truth of our being can only be pointed to using analogy, poetry and parables.

From this stillness, I will describe the world of apparent forms – the things and events that we are all familiar with – the world of 'I am'. If I asked 'who are you?' you might say *'I am ....'* and give your name, your age, your relationships to others, your profession and perhaps your likes and dislikes. All these descriptions are the 'I am' – they are who you believe you are not *what* you are. In truth, you are the impersonal 'I' before naming. The 'I am' is the illusionary Self, the conditioned mind – *who you believe you are*. Virtually all your suffering is born from misidentification with this illusionary Self.

Who you are suffers – what you are does not. Therefore, when the illusion is revealed who you believe you are disappears along with its suffering.

I will point to your true nature, to the core of your being – *the I before I am*. There will be no building of ideas and concepts culminating throughout the book; instead, I will try to reveal this ground of being with every word I write. Because it is difficult to see the illusion of the Self when you are in it, I will give analogies and poems to point to it, some of which are from ancient texts others are my own.

First, let us see if we can close in on *the I before I am* by questioning your Self: So what exactly is the innermost essence that is the unchanging part of you? What appears to give you continuity over time – what is the constant? It cannot be your thoughts because they continually change; appearing and disappearing like the wind. It cannot be your memory as that fades and distorts, it cannot be your concepts or the people you know because again these are in constant flux. Your loved ones may give you a strong sense of identity, but that reassurance is from their perspective and comes from outside. It cannot be your emotions because they come and go too and are ever changing, as are your preferences, nor can it be your body because that is temporary and all its cells are replaced as it ages. All these things are fleeting forms and as such, they are finite and temporary. However, there is something (although not a thing) that holds all these changing forms – a stillness within.

This stillness at your core is the impersonal awareness that comes before *I am* – it is the source of all things. It is not your thoughts or the story they create. For the enlightened, it is what awakens from the dream of you, but whether enlightened or unenlightened you are it and it is you.

❦

All our suffering comes from the belief that the Self is real, when in fact the Self is both real and unreal, and therefore our suffering is both real and unreal. To clarify; by 'Self' I am referring to our personal identity: 'myself', 'my mind', 'my persona', 'my character', 'my consciousness', 'my name', 'my story', 'my thoughts', 'me'. The Self is real in the sense that within the illusion of the conditioned mind everything in our lives seems very important and very real, as does our suffering. It is unreal when it is realised that we falsely identify as a Self with a personal story. To see though the illusion of the Self and its story and to see the world as it is, rather than as we would like it to be, is Enlightenment. Life is then no longer a projection of our illusionary Self with its story of how things should be; instead, it is accepted as it is without conflict and therefore without suffering. Life becomes so simple without carrying the burden of a personal story. However, there is no path leading to this emancipation because taking paths in an attempt to reach goals simply adds to the personal story and strengthens the illusionary Self. No one can lead you to this way of perceiving; I can lay the groundwork by focusing on the illusion of the Self, but glimpses of your true nature are down to grace – when you are ready, they will happen. There is no path to Enlightenment.

We know when we are happy and content and at peace, and we know when we are unhappy, sad and depressed. At times of happiness, peace and contentment we are free from stress, but it is difficult to hold onto these feelings of wellbeing because sooner or later (usually sooner) negative thoughts arrive and the peace is shattered. Therefore, our happiness is always temporary because it is based upon thoughts that can change in an instant. Nevertheless, in those brief moments of quiet peacefulness, we get a flavour of what life could be like, and we want more of the same. We try all our lives to find peace and happiness, but it is a continual effort trying to balance all the areas of our lives so we can feel happy rather than worried and concerned. Just as one area of our life falls into place, another problem arises. We are like jugglers spinning plates – all our concentration and energies are focused on keeping them in the air, our only respite is in that brief time when they are all balanced and in motion, but even then it is stressful as we fret about which plate will topple next.

The happiness, peace and contentment we experience when our thoughts are stress free is fleeting and is not freedom from suffering. It is a superficial and temporary relief from our deeper worries and concerns, in the same way that those who turn to alcohol and other drugs find only temporary respite – when the effects wear off they are faced with the same problems. Whereas when we see through the illusionary Self we can face life as it happens in the moment – there is no need to escape, we simply notice thoughts and feelings arising rather than becoming them. (This should not to be confused with a forced detachment from life whereby we make a conscious decision to deny our feelings in order to self protect). This subtle change will dramatically affect our lives because we will perceive from a clear, unfiltered perspective. From this new open space, we feel connected to everyone and everything around us because we are living in openness and honesty rather than from a constricted and defensive self-centeredness. This new perspective reveals how the habits of building and maintaining defences and interacting from a fixed idea of 'I am' creates the false Self and its suffering. This Self is sustained and validated by our story, which is constantly referenced as we go about our daily lives. We attack anything that threatens our ideas and understandings of who we are; we would rather keep our misery than lose our Self.

Most of us live our lives believing our stories, but when it is realised that the Self is an illusion those stories collapse and a clarity and stillness sets us free from the bonds of our past and the fear of the future. Afterwards we reside in the only reality that exists: the present moment – *the I before I am*. We no longer struggle to fit the reality of 'what happens' into what we think should happen because there is no story telling us how things should be. We still apparently act in the world but action flows through us from a deeper being-ness; we apparently plan and make decisions but not out of fear or worry because our constant mind chatter has been silenced. We find ourselves in the world but not of the world, we are no longer in conflict with what is – we are in tune with what is. In fact, more accurately, it is recognised that the 'Self' we thought we were never existed and what remains is what was always there – the stillness beneath that cannot be harmed. The recognition that the Self is illusionary ends our suffering.

3
MY 'STORY'

... and never have I felt so deeply at one and the same time so detached from myself and so present in the world.

ALBERT CAMUS

I have had no epiphany, no moment of Liberation or Enlightenment, and no transformational 'before and after' event. There is just an awareness (*apparently deepening over time*) that each moment of conscious experience is not my experience, and that consciousness itself, although appearing to be limited and personal, is in fact, infinite and impersonal.

It is only in recent years that I have started to understand and articulate this awareness. I have spent the vast majority of my life as a quiet introspective loner and to some extent have remained so. Life was very confusing as a teenager and young adult, because I found it hard to form and maintain a personal identity – a Self. I found it incredibly difficult to articulate my thoughts and feelings regarding this, and so from an early age I looked to philosophy and psychology for answers; I felt there was nothing inside me, and thought finding a core concept could give me a reality – something I could hold on to and call 'myself'. In the absence of a centre, I believed the only way I could function was to mirror other people by setting myself goals and by trying to engage with what I perceived as life's trivialities – hardly surprising then that I felt like an 'outsider', observing life in a detached way rather than actively engaging with it.

While most young people were out enjoying life I withdrew into a world of books immersing myself in psychology and philosophy, both ancient and modern, looking for parallels to how I was experiencing things and trying to make sense of my life. As the years passed and life played its song I did my best to join in, but my song always sounded out of tune. After a generally miserable time in high school I muddled through University, and then spent decades in IT jobs, none of which I enjoyed. In my mid-twenties, I married and several years later started a family. I followed a career path I disliked in order to support the life I had chosen. Decades of working in the wrong environment was soul destroying – I never felt at ease, even at home I often felt like an outsider and I realised philosophy had become my refuge. However, intellectual understandings were ultimately unsatisfying; there was always something I could not put my finger on – something within, untouched by external events or intellectual insights, a sort of detached witnessing. It took until middle age before I focussed seriously upon Eastern philosophy and spirituality – specifically the Hindu philosophy of Advaita. I had touched upon other traditional Indian teachings years earlier flirting with Buddhism for a time, but it did not appeal to me back then. However, once I had immersed myself in the perennial wisdom of Advaita something clicked – I found a deep resonance with my own experience and I was to spend the next decade exploring traditional and contemporary Advaita teachings and their teachers.

The word Advaita translates as non-dual or 'not two', and I found something at the heart of this ancient philosophy that struck a chord in me. I began to understand my own living experience retrospectively through it. I began to see why throughout my life virtually every surface level drama being played out seemed false and insignificant. Despite feeling somewhat detached, this was not a nihilistic or pessimistic disposition that haunted my inner world but rather an inability to reconcile that inner world with the outer world. In hindsight, it is not surprising that others found it difficult to understand me – I found it difficult to understand me! What I now seemed to be experiencing – *and had experienced sporadically throughout my life* – was what many spiritual teachers were pointing to throughout the ages: an indescribable being-ness wherein the individual events in life are seen as impermanent ripples on the surface of a deep eternal stillness. I felt I was a relative manifestation of that stillness. In philosophical terms this would be comparable to the metaphysics of Monism: the view that reality is one unitary organic whole with no independent parts, and also Panpsychism: the view that consciousness is a universal and primordial feature of all things (discussed further in Chapter 12). *'The world you perceive is made of consciousness: what you call matter is consciousness itself'* (Nisargadatta Maharaj).

However, for many years, I still had one foot firmly planted in the illusion and this caused me great suffering. There were moments of deep peace and clarity, but these were always fleeting because my thoughts would kick in attempting to understand and personalise the experience – 'thinking' literally ran away with me protecting and strengthening the illusion of my Self. I found it increasingly difficult to reconcile what I sensed as the truth of my existence with the pressures of my practical life and my personal relationships, and no doubt appeared distant and detached even to those close to me. Then came a sort of crash in my personal life as my marriage ended and my career stumbled and I found myself in a different environment where the philosophy and the metaphysics could flourish and where, for the first time in my life, it felt natural to express my inner world and where my philosophical and metaphysical thoughts and feelings were reciprocated. Several years later, on New Year's Day 2012, I decided to write down all my thoughts. I gathered all the scribbled notebooks I had filled over the years and transferred them to my computer. In the process of transcribing my notes and with a new understanding of the ancient texts, I began to find clarity of thought that enabled me to re-evaluate how I had been experiencing the world throughout my life. I came to realise that this feeling of detachment, of being an 'outsider', was born from an inexpressible awareness and that my true nature existed at a deeper level, there was a sense that I needed to somehow step aside to allow this deeper truth to surface. Over the following years, my awareness deepened and my writing developed and shaped into a book I felt could connect with a wide readership. By questioning commonly held beliefs I hope my readers can transcend their limited Self concepts and realise their individual personas are created thorough a lifetime of conditioning, producing a dream character that believes in a personal story.

There are no doubt many lost souls out there, outsiders who feel a deep disconnection and dissatisfaction with their lives – you may be one of them, perhaps sensing there is something fundamentally wrong and feeling your life is somehow false or illusionary. You may also feel worn down by the insanity of constant overthinking in a hopeless attempt to make sense of the world and your place within it. I came to see that what we have been taught and accepted as truths (discussed further in Chapter 15) are in fact a product of a shared illusion and that it is our thoughts that create our suffering and perpetuate the illusion. In an attempt to reveal the shared illusion and the thoughts that sustain it, I have written this uncompromising exploration into the heart of your existence that questions any notions you have of being a separate Self. By exposing this illusion, the division between 'you' (the apparent subjective perceiver) and 'not you' (the world of seemingly independent objective phenomena) may collapse, leaving in its wake an impersonal awareness arising from the eternal Absolute. This ever-present awareness is the stillness underlying all phenomena including you: the unifying core reality from which everything appears – *the I before I am.*

4
THE SELF

The true value of a human being can be found in the degree to which he has attained liberation from the self.

ALBERT EINSTEIN

It may be that the satisfaction I need depends on my going away, so that when I've gone and come back, I'll find it at home.

RUMI

THE SELF

The Self wants to be happy, peaceful and content. It seeks clarity, peace of mind and an end to its suffering. It wants to escape from the daily struggle, to stop simply surviving and to start living, free from self-doubt, anxiety and fear. It wants life to unfold naturally and to embrace uncertainty, change and the unknown, and live the truth, and for life to reflect back that truth. It wants to feel at peace and at one with others, to be free from the fear of death and the constriction it places upon life. It wants to be free from stressful thoughts and live in a still mind. Rather than trying to satisfy these desires, we need to recognise where they come from – we need to turn inwards because looking externally cannot fulfil these wishes (discussed further in Chapter 6). By repeatedly focusing attention within, this book aims to expose as an illusion that which desires these things, and in so doing free you from your Self.

In your life, you will have been encouraged to embrace the Self through sayings such as *believe in yourself and anything's possible*, which is usually offered as a panacea to self-doubt and lack of confidence. However, such seemingly encouraging statements are part of the reason you find yourself on life's treadmill as *I did*, desiring all manner of things and finding fulfilment in none. Many believe an alternate to believing in one's Self is surrendering to a higher power, and some religions offer this through the union with God. Belief in God through faith promises salvation and everlasting life, but such apparent surrender can imprison and increase suffering if it comes from a self-fulfilling need – in other words, if it is used to feed the yearnings of the illusionary Self, which unfortunately is usually the case. Surrender, in the truest sense, is dis-identification with the egoic mind and the collapse of the illusionary Self. Therefore, the truth of your being is not about intellectual conviction or having faith in divinities, nor it is about believing in your Self or in God; it is about relaxing the grip on your story, and resting for a moment between past and future, free from the shackles of history and hope. It is about taking your foot off the gas and slowly coasting to a stop so that you can rest in the eternal present. Then from that place of pure being, life will flow through you and its unrestricted freedom will open up infinite new possibilities enriching your life and the lives of those around you.

You are not the Self. The Self is a mirage arising from misidentification and the accompanying need to take ownership of life. You are *that* which comes before identification and ownership; you are *that* which gives rise to all. If you breathe in the emptiness of non-Self, then the struggle to control and manipulate will fall away as the external forms merge with the stillness inside, and the stillness inside merges with the external forms.

The true Self is the stillness within – *the Absolute* – the underlying awareness that is open to everything and everyone. Any thoughts that arise cannot touch this; it cannot be harmed or changed. Seeing through the illusion of your Self by gradually dropping your attachment to thoughts will expose all your desires, fears and anxieties as irrelevant background noise, causing ripples through an otherwise still and silent void and the difficulties of the human condition will begin to fall away. With the death of the Self the fear of mortality drops away, as does the need to follow others. For those of a religious nature who are egoically led, the pillars of faith and belief that support religious dogma will also crumble. Your isolated persona will diminish, and the feeling of unease created by living under the tyranny of self-doubt, guilt and uncertainty will lift, along with the incessant need to self-protect. The puffed up ego deflates like a seeping balloon as the air that gave it form returns to the unrestricted and limitless expanse from which it came. Your defences lower because there is nothing left to defend and all divisions fade as the bounded separateness of the constricted Self disperses back into the boundless Absolute.

❧

No one can show you the truth. The truth is not yours to embrace or mine to offer. I have found that it is truth that embraces all. The wave does not manifest the ocean – the ocean manifests the wave, and as both wave and ocean are one body, so too are all apparent forms but one truth. This cannot be captured – I do not have it. Those who think it can be possessed, have either misperceived its essence or been schooled into believing it can be owned and utilised through the ego. We have all witnessed the madness, misery and suffering that ensues when truth, as in some religions, becomes monopolised, zealous and prescriptive.

Discarding religious dogmatism and following alternative spiritual paths as a means to an end will advance you no further. Such spiritual pursuits neither progress nor edify the illusionary Self; it is the notion of seeking from a false perspective that is flawed – the methods are irrelevant. Whether your intellect is fully engaged or your mind supposedly emptied, it is seeking that creates a world of duality as it breathes life into your illusionary Self. As for the atheist who shuns spirituality and denies the existence of God, Enlightenment and Liberation, I suggest taking a step back and questioning the existence of *that* which believes it is an atheist. This message may actually favour the atheist/non-believer, since they are free from the added complexity of a faith based on an illusionary egoic Self – a faith that ostensibly surrenders to a higher power while covertly pandering to the individual's needs and desires.

I am not promising spiritual nirvana or a framework upon which to build an intellectual understanding, rather, I am attempting to point to your inherent emptiness by showing that you are not your thoughts, but rather the awareness that holds the thoughts. *'It takes a little time to create a gap between the witness and the mind – once the gap is there, you are in for a great surprise, that you are not the mind, you are the witness, a watcher'* (Osho). You are the eternal witness – a truth the Self will find difficult to envisage and impossible to know, as naming falsifies it. I have found that the biggest impediment to knowing the truth of one's existence is to seek it from the perspective of the illusionary Self. For the truth to flower the seeker must collapse. It is absurd to search for a truth you are immersed in, and those who do so are like fish swimming around in search of water. Simply being with *what is* removes the need to seek anything else and negates the Self, something I will discuss in the chapters to come.

❖

In summary then, seekers believe attaining spiritual goals will bring perpetual bliss, peace and happiness, but coveting them only anchors the individual firmly within the illusion and the goals become distant mirages. Contrary to what one might assume, the Absolute is not an omnipotent force for good, accessible to only the virtuous, who then channel it into right thought and right action. The Absolute is impersonal and therefore not something the Self can gain or make use of. This message is not about personal gain; rather, it is about loss – the loss of your Self. A person totally identified with the Self lives an egoic life of fear and desire; nevertheless, even within this turmoil of needy fulfilment there is often an inexplicable drive to live a virtuous life of meaning and purpose. The less one identifies with the Self the more opportunity there is for virtue to flower naturally rather than being artificially cultivated, and therefore the less harm one can do to oneself and to others. If there is little or no identification with the Self then there is virtually no egoic motivation as you are acting through pure presence, which in the truest sense is unconditional love. True love is selfless – love without a Self. From that place, no harm can be done; in fact, you live in harmony with what is and are therefore open to new possibilities that will enrich your life.

Whether this book has the potential to expose the illusion of the Self, laying bare the ground of your being and illuminating the emptiness at your core is questionable; however, the fact is I have no choice other than to be writing it, just as you have no choice other than to be reading it. You may disagree, but the infinitely complex chain of events that have resulted in this writing, and your equally complex history that has brought you to this precise moment could not have been any different. The fact that we are connecting through these words may seem like random chance, but this is the natural unfolding of what 'is', wherein all the apparent events in our lives could not have unfolded any differently. So, having arrived here through the convergence of our respective histories, *whether you believe it is predestined or not*, let us examine the Self together.

5
THE ILLUSION

It is all the mind can do – discover the unreal as unreal.
The problem is only mental, abandon false ideas, that is all.
There is no need of true ideas. There aren't any.

NISARGADATTA MAHARAJ

Losing an illusion makes you wiser than finding a truth.

LUDWIG BÖRNE

THE ILLUSION

I would like you to imagine a magic show, but not the traditional kind of performance. There is a stage magician surrounded by props, standing before an expectant audience, but instead of trying to amaze and bewilder using smoke and mirrors, he intends to reveal the illusions one by one as the performance unfolds: showing the sleight of hand, the misdirection, the trap door and the hidden compartments. So rather than heavily draped velvet curtains, mood lighting and atmospheric music, the curtains are drawn back, the music is killed and the stage lighting is turned up. Accustomed as they are to being deceived, the audience find this disconcerting. They expect to see the impossible made possible, although not actually believing in magic they want to experience it nonetheless. The audience are an integral and crucial part of the whole charade, because without them, there would be no observers and therefore no magic.

As this particular performance unfolds, the magician wastes no time in explaining how the illusions are designed and executed. Watching in silence, the audience experience mixed emotions: on the one hand, fascination and astonishment at the ingenuity and subtlety employed in the deception, but on the other, a feeling of loss, because the magic has been killed in the process. The magician continues to reveal the illusions one by one: showing the trick padlocks, the fake handcuffs and the assistant's twin, until eventually, the audience have seen through them all. The performance is not what the audience wanted; they may have been entertained but not in the manner they were expecting. The interesting thing is that whereas a traditional magic show can be enjoyed many times over, once this particular performance ends there is no interest in seeing it again. Once the illusions are exposed, the show's over.

As you read on you may have certain expectations, hoping for an intoxicating mixture of insights and truths, or perhaps a new perspective on life that could lead to a personal transformation – a desire to rise above everyday concerns, easing your pain and suffering. Perhaps even a chance to win that elusive golden ticket to Enlightenment. First, you must come to understand as I did that chasing these goals from within the illusion takes you further from them. Such dualistic thinking simply buys into the illusion. There is already a deep peace waiting to be discovered here and now, all that is required is a shift in perspective that allows you to see through the illusion. However, for me to reveal that the idea you have of your Self is a misperception will not be as simple as exposing a trap door or a sleight of hand trick. This is because your existence as a separate individual appears to be self-evident; most people live their entire lives without questioning this, and so there are deeply ingrained thought patterns to address, which we will discuss in the coming chapters.

You are creating an illusionary Self moment to moment without realising it. No effort is required for the illusion to work because you are playing both audience and performer, observing your Self magically appearing moment by moment. The conditioning needed to sustain this charade has been programmed into the way you think (discussed further in Chapter 15), and requires very little conscious thought or consideration. The reason Enlightenment and Liberation are so appealing is that they are products of the same illusion and therefore the possibility of a higher spiritual existence taps into the story of personal fulfilment.

The message I am sharing is not about claiming for the Self a higher level of spirituality or a deeper level of consciousness; it is about a very subtle shift in perspective that exposes an illusion. I have found that focusing upon your thoughts and watching them rather than becoming them brings a new lucidity to the present moment; it is comparable to turning up the lights and pulling back the curtains on the magic show. Just as the audience stop

THE ILLUSION

buying into the magic as the illusions are revealed, so I stopped buying into my thoughts as they arose. The underlying stillness then became apparent, and I saw with a clarity devoid of illusion.

The irony is that the message underlying this book is truly magical; in pure being-ness there is no deception, no illusion and no barrier between reality and the so called 'me'; the 'individual' merges with reality – there is no separation. It is so obvious and simple the thought arises: *'how could this ever have been overlooked?'* followed by laughter at an illusion taken so seriously, and tears at the indescribable beauty and effortless perfection of simply being.

In certain brief moments in everyday life, you may sense, *as I did*, that something is not quite right – that there is no substance to the Self. In those moments, your life may feel like a performance read from a script you have been fed from birth. You may sense a disengagement or un-coupling from everyday life as it dawns upon you that you do not really know who or what you are, and your world momentarily blurs as everything you have taken to be real suddenly feels equally unreal, and what was very important a moment ago feels inconsequential. These moments when you lose the sharp focus of the individual Self and your familiar perspective shifts can be difficult to comprehend and extremely unsettling, and I found that self-preservation kicks in, focusing attention back to the security of the illusion.

I moved back and forth between these worlds over decades. Staying with that unsettling and incomprehensible feeling and closing in on what is essentially your nonexistence will not be easy. Regardless of how painful life often seems, you will instinctively fight to keep your Self alive – not only because you fear the alternative, but you also believe that through the Self – *through your effort* – you can find peace. In fact, these goals and desires are the cause of your suffering and keep you trapped within an illusion. By opening up to the present moment and noticing the stillness beneath the thoughts, there is a return to the immersive peace you yearn for.

❊

Searching for an ultimate reality or truth using thought simply creates more illusions, which in turn leads to disappointment and suffering. This message could alleviate such suffering, but to do so, that which suffers – the

Self – has to be seen for what it is: an illusion. However, this presents a difficulty, since it appears to be the illusionary Self that reads these words and the same Self that I am asking you to surrender. Therefore, in this respect it is like asking the thief to arrest themself.

At one level of understanding, it seems obvious that the Self exists because we accept the reality of that experience. As Descartes declared in his second meditation: *'Doubtless, then, I exist, since I am deceived; and, let him deceive me as he may, he can never bring it about that I am nothing, so long as I shall be conscious that I am something'*. To support his position of an existing Self, he stated: *'I think, therefore I am'* (The Meditations, 1639). That there is experience seems undeniable, but what I am bringing into question is who is having the experience? In other words, I am trying to separate the experience from the illusion that something – namely the constricted individual – is having it (the subjective 'I am'). The perception of a subjective 'experiencer' is illusionary, the underlying reality from which experience happens is the I before I am – the Absolute that lives through us and animates everything. However, we cannot know the Absolute because we are the Absolute and it cannot know itself – just as the hand cannot grasp itself and the eye cannot see itself.

I hope that with this understanding, you can see why I am offering you – the individual Self – very little. There are no life skills or meditation practices, no accumulative stages of understanding or ascending steps to Enlightenment. All I ask is that you put your Self under the microscope by noticing your thoughts as they arise (detailed in Chapter 7). Such scrutiny will reveal there is nothing you need to do or achieve, and no action you need to take, because there is no individual Self at your core. If this is realised - not just intellectually understood but experienced at the deepest level, then a falling away will occur in which being-ness simply happens, unfiltered by the conditioned mind. Life will then be laid bare. What remains will blossom naturally and unfold with a simple grace and beauty unencumbered and untouched by any preconceived notions of what life is or how it should be lived. Life will flow as naturally as breathing, requiring neither effort nor willpower. Those living this Truth will not benefit personally; the experience will not be theirs because it does not become part of the egoic Self. However, there will be indescribable peace out of which apparent actions arise and through which day-to-day life happens – the difference being you witness life unfolding in front of you, rather than buying into the stressful illusion that you control things.

The Absolute is beyond individual hopes and outside self-knowledge and self-improvement and yet it is closer than you could imagine – it is right here permeating every experience. You do not experience the Absolute – the Absolute experiences you. There are no Enlightened beings – just Enlightened being.

6
SPIRITUAL PATHS, EMPTINESS AND NON-SELF

In the measurement world, we set a goal and strive to achieve it. In the universe of possibility, we set the context and let life unfold.

BENJAMIN ZANDER

Arriving at one goal is the starting point to another.

JOHN DEWEY

Let us look more closely at some of the difficulties we have living our lives and why we fall into the same unhelpful patterns trying to find happiness and fulfilment.

At various times throughout your life you will have experienced periods of anxiety, frustration, extreme sadness and perhaps bouts of depression, often with a sense that something is missing or something more is needed, indeed for many people these feelings are a regular occurrence and become their daily reality. As discussed, there will no doubt be periods of contentment, happiness and peace, but these will be transient or intermittent interludes, before the turbulence of life returns. It seems that suffering and dissatisfaction are stitched into the very fabric of life. Currently, your life may be rather messy with unresolved issues, insecurities, niggling doubts and worries – a life that makes little sense, where the thoughts and actions of others are often unpredictable and confusing, and these difficulties do not just lie with others – you are probably in the habit of continually second-guessing your own thoughts, which seem overly complex and unhelpful. Therefore, you find yourself in a constant battle trying to control and make sense of what is happening. Quite naturally, you want to get to a better place, and this is why spiritual paths are so appealing – since they offer the hope that one day there will be a future free from chaos and pain, a place where life makes sense and order replaces chaos easing, if not ending, your suffering.

Reaching this utopian future is often thought to depend upon sorting out certain practical problems, thereby giving you the time, the space and the peace of mind to achieve your goals, and to sort out your life once and for all. You may reason, if you could just sort out these urgent problems first giving you some breathing space, then you would have the time to take a long hard look at your life and make some long overdue changes. However, those urgent problems never go away – they seem never-ending, and so you stumble from one crisis to another in a reactive and programmed way until the problems become your life and your life becomes a problem.

Often there is a belief that spiritual paths will enable you to break from this insanity and achieve your goal of peaceful living. This all seems perfectly plausible, since you have observed other people apparently living that reality. Consequently, you may read books by authors promising to deliver a utopian life. Studying the ideas of others, and following their paths may seem to help, providing a positive distraction from your current insufferable situation. Such practices and promises can be very appealing, and much time and effort can be spent following a path to turn your life around. However, it only takes one errant thought, triggered by an unforeseen event, for your problems to bubble back to the surface, and the raw suffering of life dumps you right back where you started.

All spiritual paths offer hope, hope that one day your mind will become settled. Hope is kept alive by beginning journeys with long timescales. Time is the great protector as it keeps the hope alive by putting distance between the current insufferable situation, and the promise of a release into future happiness. In effect, time protects you from disappointment by adding distance. Long enough timescales can give the appearance of progress and the feeling that goals are steadily approaching, allowing for setbacks, sabbaticals and second winds. However, you never quite reach your goal because the gains assumed upon arrival never materialise. You never reach that utopian dream where everything falls effortlessly into place and all your doubts and anxieties disappear, and all your desires are fulfilled. You never seem to reach a point in life where pain and suffering cease. You consequently find yourself once again confronted with your own suffering. Therefore, rather than easing your pain by investing your hopes in a spiritual path that promises happiness in the future, let's instead look at how you have arrived at this point, and then focus upon the underlying conditions of your suffering right here and right now.

We are conditioned from birth to see the world in dualistic terms, thus placing our Self as a separate entity that has to strive in the world. Our illusory perception of Self fuels our egotistical desire, where we constantly want to acquire the things that we think we need for our emotional/physical welfare. Suffering seems to come about because we refuse to accept things as they are, and persist to desire how we think things should be to satisfy our notions of happiness. As long as we believe we are a Self that needs fulfilling, we will always be cultivating an on-going dissatisfaction for our lot. In other words, as long as we perceive ourselves as a separate Self, we will be trying to quench our thirst in a whole range of ways: consumerism, achievements, career progression, relationships etc.

You may have spent years pursuing material goals, but now sense the futility of chasing such desires, and therefore your search has turned towards finding a deeper purpose to life – a higher meaning or profound truth. However, while such aspirations may at face value sound preferable to material desires, if you have nurtured such spiritual paths through intellectual investigation, meditative practices or religious devotion, you will find they are ultimately unfulfilling and, furthermore, that when the pressures of life are exerted, they desert you. It is only after the difficulties subside and the dust settles that you can regain any sense of equilibrium. There are many ways to find temporary relief from the pressures of life: Your Buddha moment may be enjoyed in the comfort and security of your home, or with a select circle of like-minded friends. You may have found a life-coach or self-help guru who seems to make sense. Giving praise at church, surrounded by the love and warmth of your fellow worshipers may bring a sense of peace and solace. You may derive a sense of harmony and a clearer understanding of the world by reading your favourite philosopher, or attain a peaceful state of mind through meditation.

Nevertheless, these experiences are short-lived and cannot be sustained when faced with real world problems where people behave in random and inconsistent ways and events are unpredictable and haphazard, where past and future invade the present moment bringing regret, anxiety and worry. Your frustration at certain situations can erupt from nowhere, and your anger can spark in an instant. Even if such emotions are internalised so as not to cause embarrassment or upset they nonetheless affect you, because suddenly and without warning your inner peace and tranquillity is shattered. It appears that your profound personal moments of quiet contemplation and deep understanding simply refuse to transfer into the cut and thrust of daily life, and you find yourself desperately trying to hold on to a faint echo of the peace you imagined was sustainable. Any deep transformative feelings of love and tranquillity, peace and serenity only seem to exist in the familiar environment of your safe haven, where you feel in control and can imagine a sense of truth and harmony.

Acknowledging the difficulty in understanding the motives and actions of others, and questioning life's adversities and inequalities, often prompts these searches for answers that transcend the apparent chaotic randomness of daily life. This creates the desire for higher spiritual awareness, a deeper meaning or transcendent philosophy – something that raises awareness and expands consciousness, giving new perspectives on life. For many, finding a clear spiritual path through life's maze using aspirational goals as an incentive seems to be the answer.

However, attempting to grow personally and spiritually by working towards goals, such as acceptance, peace, harmony, freedom, Enlightenment and Liberation is made from a reference point that does not exist. That is to say, the Self that has expectations of reaching and benefiting from such goals, is illusionary – as is the Self that apparently takes action to achieve the desired results; as is the Self that monitors progress towards such goals. When goals are supposedly reached, the satisfaction is always short-lived because there is no actual Self to benefit or find fulfilment through them. Your new spiritually enriched Self quickly returns to feeling no different from the spiritually impoverished one, as the fruits of your labour begin to fade and feel intangible, unsatisfying and hollow. In fact, all that appears to exist when any such goal is reached is a conditioned need to strive for the next.

Taking time out for contemplation, meditation or prayer can sometimes lead to moments of clarity and wisdom. These practices may bring a deeper meaning in the moment, but the challenge is always to carry those profound realisations and understandings into the turmoil of daily life in order to make sense of the outside world and to live a more harmonious life. This brings disappointment time and again, because in the midst of the chaos, there is a reoccurring frustration at the ease in which your inner peace vanishes. On venturing out into the world, your cultivated equilibrium is soon challenged and starts to unravel. Those thoughts and subsequent actions do not match your idealistic standards or spiritual aspirations, and far from transcending the chaos through a deeper understanding and calm acceptance, it is those very thoughts that add to the confusion and the frustration. You find yourself overthinking everything in an attempt to find the truth, and the more you think the more frustrated you become because instead of gaining clarity, things are less clear; like swirling a stick in a muddy pool in an attempt to see to the bottom – the action simply causes greater disturbance and murkiness.

Returning to your quiet place, a familiar and unsettling hollowness descends. This hollowness is often tinged with annoyance, and you become frustrated because you feel that you have let yourself down: how could your clarity, peace of mind and calm acceptance revert so quickly into the old knee-jerk reactions? Time and again, your thoughts and actions in the real world falsify the inner peace you believed you had found. You do not like falling into those old patterns, and you do not like the fact that certain people irritate you, and make you feel uncomfortable. Nor do you like the annoyance you feel towards them, or the anxiousness felt in their presence. You do not like the anger you feel when someone jumps the queue at the checkout or the frustration you experience when you are running late and the car in front is slowing you down. You do not like it when a family member or a close friend is unkind to you, unsympathetic to your situation, or indifferent to your feelings.

You wonder where your inner harmony and calm acceptance goes in these flashpoint moments, and why it is so difficult to sustain your goal of consistent peaceful living. Therefore, you question your resolve: perhaps your meditation is not deep enough; your spiritual understandings are not profound enough; your philosophical insights are incomplete, or your religious devotion lacks purity. You conclude you must try harder, rationalising that attaining the ultimate goal is not going to be easy, and must be worked at. Therefore, you raise the bar and the striving intensifies. You search for more obscure sages, open your heart wider to God's love, meditate deeper or seek more profound philosophies. If you are struggling with depression and low self-worth, you may fall back into old patterns and vices to numb the pain of living. You may look to distractions to fill your time through popular culture – music, film and literature, but there is always the faint hope that one day a spark will ignite your self-realisation and turn your life around.

For those committed to a spiritual path a process of incremental progression seems sensible, in the same way that you might take lessons to learn how to drive or play a musical instrument. However, making progress through practice, patience and repetition is only possible in the world of phenomena (objects in the physical world). To understand this, consider a goal such as learning to play the piano. You – a 'body –mind' (phenomena) can act upon a piano (phenomena) to learn the mechanics of playing through memory, coordination and repetition. With dedication, practice and patience, improvements can be made, and goals approached or even attained.

However, goal-oriented endeavours fail when phenomena (objects in the physical word, including *body-minds*) attempt to act upon noumena (the spiritual/non-physical or meta-physical, *that which cannot be known or perceived*). Using your intellect and working with what you believe is true to form an understanding of your relationship to others, to yourself and to the world around you, and then applying that understanding in your daily life may seem quite sensible. However, attempting to work on life as though it were a piano objectifies it into something you believe you can master. The assumption is that just as you can learn to play the piano, you can similarly learn to play life. Unfortunately, learning to play life is impossible simply because it is life that is 'playing' you. Life is the manifestation of the Absolute – an Absolute that animates everything: the source that flows through all body-minds, including you and me. You mistakenly believe the source flowing through your body-mind originates in you and is personal to you – that you are a self-directed independent entity out of which life emerges. This is the illusion of being a Self. This personalised Self vainly attempts to control and master what it believes to be its own inner source with theories, ideas, contemplations and actions. Again, all such efforts are useless; like a leaf on the surface of life's river you are carried along in the flow, you have no control over your movement.

Therefore, although certain body-minds with the right aptitude can master the piano, no amount of effort, strength of will or natural ability allows one to master life. The Self believes it is a real thing – a phenomena predicated on the perceived existence of the body-mind. Because the body-mind can apparently manipulate and master other phenomena, the Self believes it can similarly manipulate and master life. Within the illusion, this seems a sensible assumption, and is precisely why people spend a lifetime attempting to fulfil their needs and desires in a fruitless attempt to find happiness.

The illusionary Self labours under the misapprehension that it is the source of its actions and can manipulate and control life, which is analogous to the leaf in the river's flow believing it controls its own movement. The source flowing through you appears to originate from within the body-mind. The illusionary Self is born out of this misapprehension, it claims ownership thereby changing 'experience' into *your* 'experience' and distorting and filtering all sense perceptions through this erroneous perspective.

Because the illusionary Self falsely assumes life can be manipulated and controlled for its own benefit, when you are presented with life's seemingly insurmountable problems, you instinctively want answers and set about gaining additional knowledge in order to increase understanding and find solutions. It is quite natural to ask questions and seek answers, because throughout life you have been fed questions and taught the answers; having answers feels satisfying and gives a sense of security and control. Furthermore, doing things in the world of phenomena appears to bring results, such as learning to play the piano, but you cannot apply the same rationale to tame and understand life. The illusionary Self cannot touch life let alone control it.

❊

Trying to control the flow of life is ultimately a hollow endeavour. The following analogy highlights how life flows freely and is unmoved by your efforts to exploit its force. The waterwheel turns due to the river's flow. The river knows nothing of this; its essence remains untouched. You mistakenly believe that you have autonomy, that you are the prime mover in your story. You believe that you are a waterwheel turning by its own volition, but you are not the prime mover or the master of your destiny. The waterwheel has no inherent power or movement of its own; its structure allows the potential for movement, but only through the river's flow. By trying to shape life and control your destiny, you are mistakenly attempting to take ownership of life, which is analogous to the waterwheel trying to change the essence of the river. Attempting to harness life's force to your own advantage is as futile as the wheel attempting to alter the river's flow. You are not the Self. You are the one Absolute, the eternal flow that moves all.

You are functioning on autopilot with a programmed set of ideas/beliefs that are never questioned (discussed further in Chapter 15). These beliefs are the various ways in which you have been conditioned to think, and the resulting thought patterns that continually monitor and control who you think you are, and what you believe is expected of you. These patterns create a strong sense of Self, a Self that you are encouraged to believe in. Self-belief is promoted as the springboard to all success and, unsurprisingly, is the main ingredient in most self-help books and motivational speeches. However, very few ask why self-belief is assumed beneficial, or why admitting a lack of it necessitates pity. Self-belief is a fixed set of defined thought patters that constrain and restrict the infinite potential within you creating a narrow, blinkered and contracted version of yourself. It is belief in the Self and the ingrained thought patterns underpinning it that imprisons you and creates your suffering. Those thoughts provide a framework for the illusionary Self, a framework that is immensely strong and built from a lifetime of conditioning from parents, teachers and peers. A framework reinforced by the need for acceptance, and made infinitely stronger by a whole network of other illusionary selves. Our conditioning may differ in many ways, however we all understand and accept the common ground rules of believing we are one of countless separate individuals, each endowed with a unique soul or essence, and each exercising free will (discussed in Chapter 17). This wider network is the society in which we live, together with the customs, traditions and behaviours it cultivates. Your current thought patterns underpinned by this framework define and sustain who you believe you are.

I refer to, for example, the thoughts that tie you up in complex mind games, such as trying to guess someone else's opinion of you and what they may or may not be thinking. These thoughts replay repeatedly in your mind, cutting ever-deeper channels into your behaviour patterns. Over time, such insecurities can become second nature, spinning into a complex web of anxieties and doubts, and you begin second-guessing every personal interaction with countless ifs, buts and maybes. Constant worry and concern over what others may be thinking, or how you believe you should respond, or what is expected of you in various situations, will take its toll both mentally and physically. You will also have expectations of others – wanting them to behave and react in ways that make sense to you. An accumulation of these thought processes over decades, along with all the anxiety caused by trying to change things that you cannot change and control things you cannot control, places a strain on your mental and physical wellbeing. Ill health has many causes but stress caused by unnecessary psychological suffering can be a huge contributory factor in undermining a healthy body. If the body is allowed to function naturally, free from the stranglehold of the illusionary Self with its expectations and demands, it will fall into the natural rhythm of life. Indeed, if left alone the body has a natural intelligence that is far superior to the intellect of the mind (discussed further in Chapter 13).

Living in the stillness of non-Self is having a deeply felt sense – *at a level beyond intellectual knowledge* – that you are the river not the waterwheel. Emptiness refers to the river: the unknowable, boundless and infinite source that animates everything, including you and me – empty of meaning or purpose and bursting with an energetic life force. My waterwheel analogy separates the wheel from the river in order to explain the illusion of an autonomous separate 'you', and how the underlying Absolute animates it, but actually, there is no separation. There is just the Absolute, the unrestricted source of all things manifesting all phenomena – *the known and the formed*, and all noumena – *the unknown and the formless*. Enlightenment is intuiting that there is no separation between you and the underlying source. Such a realisation liberates you from the huge burden of believing you are a constricted, self-governing, mind-body that must constantly Self protect and control the world around you. However, Enlightenment is not some 'thing' to reach for and to attain – it is about letting go, because striving for it reinforces the notion that you are an individual Self that can take action, such as taking steps towards becoming Enlightened. The problem with spiritual paths is that they are as illusionary as the seekers who follow them – ironically, only the illusionary Self can follow such paths. The Self is like a particular species of shark – it has to keep moving to stay alive, the dilemma you face is that to lose your Self in the Absolute the illusionary Self must come to a standstill. Once the Self stops perpetuating its own illusion, life will have a lighter, less restricted feel – your old tunnel vision will be shattered, leaving a wide open vista, and life will return to the playground of your childhood.

7
YOU ARE NOT WHAT YOU THINK

Can you coax your mind from its wanderings and keep to the original oneness?

TAO TE CHING

Imagine a large transparent plastic box filled with hundreds of multi-coloured marbles, its high sides contain the marbles ten deep. It rests on an even bigger glass topped table in a dark windowless room and a powerful up light is placed under the table. As the light shines through the glass it is filtered through the box of marbles sending up multi-coloured rays – reds, blues, greens, yellows and purples. The colours are eye-catching, however, you want to experience the pure light source, therefore in order for the light to shine through unfiltered you part the marbles with your hands so that the bottom of the box is exposed and the rays of light can shine through. However, as soon as you take your hands away the marbles rush to fill the gap and the light is once again filtered through them.

The multi-coloured marbles are your thoughts filtering the light of pure awareness and catching your attention with their bright colours; the act of parting them is the method given later in this chapter that allows the pure light beneath to shine through. Continuing with the analogy, initially, it is quite tricky parting the marbles because they overrun your hands and backfill the space as quickly as you create it, however, with practice you are able to perfect your technique and can spread the marbles and hold the space for longer periods. Over time, something else begins to happen: the plastic box begins to expand – its sides start to stretch and its surface area increases. As the box grows, the marbles thin out until their density reduces to the point where they are no longer ten deep, but are now single marbles rolling around the bottom of the spacious box. There are just as many marbles but the space they were contained within has expanded and the light now shines through unfiltered. The expanding box is the stillness increasing within you; thoughts remain but they no longer filter the light into colours that grab your attention.

※

Let us try to expose your illusionary Self by allowing your thoughts to arise without attaching to them. By not imbibing your thoughts with a life of their own, the undefined undercurrent of what 'is' – *the I before I am* – may gradually swell and spill over into your perception of reality, washing it away and laying bare the ground of your being. As previously discussed, this being-ness is something so ordinary, closer than you could imagine but obscured by the illusionary Self.

Most people do not look beyond the surface dramas of their lives for fear of what their curiosity might uncover. Instead, they pursue countless distractions in a never-ending search for fulfilment, and as life unfolds feel they are running out of time and perhaps that they are still in ignorance of their true nature. Socrates boldly declared *The unexamined life is not worth living*, however, for most people there seems to be a reluctance, born out of fear and conditioning, to look within. By becoming aware of your conditioning and ignoring the distractions then your background, social status, academic standing, ethnicity, age, occupation, gender, appearance and predilections, all become secondary and only relatively important. Your primary reality becomes the background awareness – the Absolute from which these temporary forms arise.

To allow the possibility of the Absolute becoming your primary reality – in other words, to allow the possibility of you transcending your thought based consciousness, I will move away from an intellectual / philosophical discussion regarding the nature of the Self and introduce a practical way of allowing you to start noticing your thoughts rather than becoming them. I am of course suggesting a technique here and therefore it is as much a part of the illusion as the Self it is trying to expose. However, consider it a thorn to remove a thorn – if it does its job and the illusionary Self is exposed then the method can also be discarded. If successful, it will appear to separate you from thoughts produced by the conditioned mind – there will be awareness of thoughts coming and going but no attaching to them. This will be a shift from total identification with thought to witnessing thought. From this new perspective, you will be able to watch thoughts arise and dissipate with detached curiosity and mild amusement.

The illusionary thorn I am suggesting you use is the statement: 'I transcend this'. Sounds simple I know, however, these three words could be the catalyst that allows you to begin to separate from your stressful and unhelpful thoughts and to witness them rather than become them. I have called it a statement, but if you find it works, then over time it will become more of a mantra. By repeating it to yourself when stressful, worrying or anxious thoughts arise you will begin the process of separating from those thoughts – of dis-identifying with them. Now before we continue it is important to dispel any suggestion that this is denying how you are feeling or changing or blocking your thinking, nor is it about altering behaviour – *although that may be a side effect*; it is simply watching these manifestations and recognising and becoming aware that the vast majority of your thoughts are negative, unhelpful and untrue and that you are the ground of being beneath them. They are nothing more than brightly coloured collections of past memories and unreal projections that grab your attention and collectively become your story, they have little to do with this present moment of being alive – in fact they kill the beauty of the present moment.

The survival of the egoic Self depends upon constant storytelling, and the narrator is thought. Children sometimes feel agitated or frightened listening to their favourite fairy tales and have to be reassured that they are not real. This method is a reassurance for the adult mind – it does not silence the narrator, but rather listens with intrigue and detachment as you would to any fictional story. No matter how real the story sounds, it never becomes your reality.

I suggest that you start with small irritations or annoyances and only tackle the bigger issues when you have tasted success with the minor ones.

As with any skill, mastery will take practice. Initially, separating from even the mildest concern will not be easy because the thought and the associated stressful feelings will appear to be one and the same, but actually they are two distinct things. So, when a stressful or disquieting thought arises repeat to yourself: 'I transcend this'. Let us look then at how most of us live our lives, focusing upon one or two practical examples and see how *I transcend this* can begin an enquiry that enables you to witness stressful thoughts, to stop identification with them and thus remove the stress. This first example is a specific work based scenario, however the same principle applies to virtually any type of public speaking.

Stressful thoughts often have a trigger. So for instance, you may be nervous about talking in a team meeting at work. Let us suppose you have to give a brief project update to the group and are conscious of a tight knot in your stomach as the meeting gets underway. You are aware of your pulse racing and feeling hot as your turn to talk approaches, and you find yourself rehearsing your words and not listening to what others are saying. It is likely that while rehearsing in your mind you lose your train of thought and start to panic about doing so when speaking. Your mouth becomes dry and you berate yourself for not remembering to bring water. Then you suddenly hear your name and realise the chair is asking for your update, and so you immediately start talking as if on autopilot. As the words come out you feel almost disembodied – you feel ill at ease and self-conscious, you may avoid eye contact with your colleagues and find yourself stumbling over certain words or phrases and focusing on those errors, hoping to god you are making sense. You feel hot and clammy as you furtively glance around the table for reassurance, but all you get back are blank expressions, which add to your anxiety. Once you have raced through your monologue and its over to the next person you feel huge relief and just hope you did not sound too muddled or nervous. Before discussing how *I transcend this* can be applied to this specific scenario, let us look at another example that shows how what you perceive is filtered by your individual story and thereby distorts the reality of the situation.

At a mindfulness retreat listening to a guest speaker discussing meditative practices I may have the thought 'What an eloquent speaker'. The speaker is the stimulus, the thought 'What an eloquent speaker' is my response;

there is little I can do about either the stimulus or my initial response. The thought is taken into my personal story and triggers other thoughts and associated feelings. Let us suppose my next thought is 'I wish I could speak as eloquently', followed by associated feelings of inferiority tinged with jealously. These feelings are my story. I have taken the initial stimulus – *experiencing an eloquent speaker*, and lost its essence by filtering it through my story. My thoughts have killed the beauty of that moment and turned it into an unpleasant feeling.

At the same retreat listening to the same speaker you may have the thought 'Very polished, but I'm not buying it', believing it sounds over rehearsed and lacks authenticity. Your irritation and scepticism comes from your story with its superior knowledge. The point is, the thought triggers a feeling, and the feeling comes from your story and therefore strengthens your illusionary Self. If you do not like the feeling, you do not like your Self, and that is stressful. It would not be so bad if most of our thoughts triggered positive feelings; unfortunately, the opposite is usually the case. We love to criticise and find fault in others, in ourselves and in our surroundings, and by doing so we miss the beauty of the present moment and indeed the valuable experience of others. I am not suggesting that you can become purely objective and suddenly stop judging people and situations; I am simply asking you to be aware of the automatic thoughts that arise and not let them runway with you.

We can break the pattern of these stressful feelings with *I transcend this*, which interrupts the thought process and allows the stimulus to be met with clarity before it is filtered through the conditioned mind. If we respond to the stimulus with the thought 'What an eloquent speaker' and can stay in that moment without feeding it into our personal story we can embrace the beauty of presence. *I transcend this* can be applied to any negative thoughts that arise, such as 'I wish they would …' or '… I wish I could …', or judgments such as 'I would have …' or 'They should have …' By acknowledging *I transcend this*, you are interrupting your conditioned thought patterns and staying in the present moment – you are staying with the raw reality of present awareness. Hence, the present moment is not made ugly by your judging mind; your personal story is severed from that moment of perception and therefore so too are any negative feelings, such as inferiority or superiority. By staying in the moment and not spinning it into your story, you will feel more connected to what is happening. You will be experiencing a very rare thing: living in the beauty of present awareness, and this can become addictive. As you begin to stay present rather than falling into your mentally constructed story, you will feel lighter and more at peace. You will feel a kind of liberation; in fact, you will start to welcome situations that previously caused anxiety, irritation and anger because they become opportunities to experience presence. *I transcend this* gives you an alternative perspective to consider and can bring the background awareness to the foreground by jolting you out of your reactive thought patterns.

In the first example concerning public speaking, your anxiety builds prior to the team meeting. This is due to past experience and the associated feelings of discomfort. Therefore, each time a team meeting comes around you feel the same anxiety. Because the event and your thoughts about it are strongly linked, as soon as the team debrief is mentioned a stomach churning feeling hits you even before you have consciously thought about it. Finding presence in this scenario is more difficult. It is harder to apply *I transcend this* to a strong emotional reaction because once your stomach is churning it is like shutting the proverbial stable door after the horse has bolted. Instead, feel the emotion fully – explore the exact feeling in the pit of your stomach as the team meeting approaches, or as you sit waiting to speak. Live with that feeling fully, concentrate just on the physical feeling and become fully aware of its location and intensity – bring presence to the churning stomach sensation. If you stay fully present with just the physical discomfort, eventually it will need feeding by a thought because your body can only stay in psychological discomfort for so long before it requires psychological input. In this respect, psychological pain is no different to physical pain: If your body is physically harmed, then the physical pain will have an intensity and duration corresponding to the physical stimulus, likewise, psychological pain has an intensity and duration corresponding to the psychological stimulus. So in order for the stomach churning to perpetuate you need to enter your story, the one that remembers past experiences and reminds itself that it hates pubic speaking. Once you have re-entered your story you can apply *I transcend this* to the thoughts. By realising the current thought is not your true reality you can break the cycle of thought fed feelings. Once that feedback loop is severed you can wake up once again to the present moment. (It could be that you are so overcome with anxiety and nervousness you cannot calm your physical discomfort and are not ready to practice *I transcend this* in that particular situation. For instance, experiencing acute anxiety or in extreme cases a panic attack, could be the body's way of telling you at this particular time and in your current state of consciousness, you need to remove yourself from the environment causing the stress.)

Once you begin to master *I transcend this* and can bring awareness to the present moment, you will relax into what were otherwise stressful situations. You will relax into the team-meeting environment and actually engage with your fellow colleagues. You listen to what each person has to say, welcoming each moment of the meeting without judgement, and then when it is your turn to speak, you speak from an open heart. You do not rush – you are measured, and as you speak, you find yourself looking around the table and actually connecting with the other people. You may even smile! You take pauses and actually welcome the silence, and because you are so at ease and so fully present you infect others with that presence, and they relax a little and perhaps feel more connected to you and to what you are saying. You have brought a raw reality to the table by meeting everyone in present awareness, and it's a rare thing because most if not all of the other people will be suffering the same mental anguish in varying degrees. The content of your debrief may be similar but you now have the freedom to feel the energy in the room and respond organically to others because you are talking from a place of openness and inner stillness rather than from a closed off internalised fear. Because what you say is no longer born out of fear it has an innocence and openness that others will find infectious. It does not mean you will give the perfect debrief or that your delivery will be faultless, but what you will have is present moment awareness and therefore a connectedness to everyone else.

What *I transcend this* has achieved in this example is to put you in touch with reality – the reality of the present moment without the illusion of your Self, its stories and associated fears. You are just sitting on a chair enjoying the beauty of the moment – you actually enjoy what you are saying and how you are saying it, including all its imperfections. If you stumble over a particular word or phrase, you will find it rather amusing and may even comment on the fact – either way it is no longer important. However, in practice you will probably make fewer mistakes because you will not be flustered, anxious or fearful. One mistake will no longer feed your anxiety and spiral into further blunders; it will simply be acknowledged and left behind. Your actual reality is now in full presence rather than allowing your story to run away with you through overthinking sending you into repetitious feedback loops of distorted perception. A word of warning: although your delivery will flow more naturally and, dare I say, even become an enjoyable experience, this is a pleasant by-product of your present moment awareness and should not become the goal. When present moment awareness becomes a means to an end, you are acting out of a desire to achieve something, and therefore you are living in an imaginary future and back in the game of the illusionary Self with all its hopes and fears.

You can break your conditioned thought patterns and the attachment to those thoughts and the resulting stressful feelings. It will not be easy because your egoic mind lives through the experiences and perceptions of your story with its needy and fearful script, but if you persevere and stay in the moment by repeating *I transcend this* you will begin to see with more clarity. You will notice the thoughts arising, but not become the thoughts – your experience of the present moment will not be filtered through your story, and therefore the Self is starved of its incessant and unproductive mind chatter. Once the majority of your stressful feelings have been addressed (and this will take some time), you will gain an amazing clarity and life will become so much easier; as unnecessary stress and anxiety lift, life can return to the magical experience it once was.

8
STRATEGIC MIND AND STORY MIND

In any situation, what really matters is not the situation but your state of consciousness that you bring to it.

ECKHART TOLLE

Fight with all the strength at your disposal against the idea that you are nameable and describable. You are not. Refuse to think of yourself in terms of this or that. Suffering is a call for enquiry, all pain needs investigation.

NISARGADATTA MAHARAJ

The examples in the previous chapter introduced *I transcend this* as a method for you to try, but I reiterate that this method is rooted firmly within the illusion, in other words it is a concept for the illusionary Self to make use of – a thorn to remove a thorn. It is not mastering or taming life; it is simply an attempt to begin quietening your mind by highlighting unhelpful and negative thought patterns. It is not showing your true nature; rather, it allows you to become aware of the frosted glass that obscures it – it exposes the filters through which you perceive. Awakening to your true nature happens through grace, not through methodologies. One could therefore ask why bother with a method or for that matter any spiritual practice? There is a Zen saying: Enlightenment is an accident, spiritual practice simply makes us accident-prone.

Within the ego drama we call life we do not truly see or hear because our story filters our perceptions. *I transcend this* severs the 'story – thought – feeling – story' feedback loop, it gives you the chance to see and hear for the first time by becoming aware of the Self and its story. Over time, the clarity that comes from applying the method will open up a completely new world of experiencing. To be able to see people and listen to them with openness and lucidity, unencumbered by judgments, values and projections, is a joy not only for you, but also for them. With your newfound clarity, you will interact with others in such a simple and uncomplicated way that all exchanges will become light and stress-free. *If you close your mind in judgements and traffic with desires, your heart will be troubled. If you keep your mind from judging and aren't led by the senses, your heart will find peace* (Tao Te Ching).

Thoughts and thinking have their place – I am not suggesting that you simply observe all your thoughts and do nothing with them; clearly, you could not function in the world with that rationale. There are infinite practical situations where thought and thinking are required and this type of 'necessary' thinking comes from what I call the Strategic Mind. For example, planning a journey, organising an event, or preparing for a presentation. The negative, unhelpful and anxiety generating thought patterns discussed in the previous chapter come from what I call the Story Mind. It is important to recognise these two distinct types of thought. Of course, it is very easy for the Strategic Mind to slip into the Story Mind, for example, you may be planning a presentation and rather that working on its content you start worrying about its delivery. Here your Strategic Mind has been high-jacked by your Story Mind and you can quickly disappear down the rabbit hole of self-obsessed and stressful thinking.

The Story Mind can of course include positive thoughts – happy stories, and for those who entertain mainly those, life can appear a lot pleasanter. Within the illusion, one could see how positive thoughts with happy stories are preferable to negative thoughts with sad stories; indeed, this is why self-help books are so popular. They work on the premise that everyone wants to turn his or her sad story into a happy one. What is not realised is that both are illusionary, which is borne out time and again when the happy story fades and begins to feel hollow and once again you begin searching for a new happy story that fulfils you. If you rely on your Story Mind to make you feel happy you are also at its mercy to make you feel sad. *I transcend this* can be applied to positive thoughts too, showing how you fall into the illusion of temporary happiness.

Now if you try to imagine seeing through the illusion of both your negative and positive thoughts you would be forgiven for picturing some sort of detached zoned-out approach to life – a kind of zombie-like existence. However, when you begin to see through the illusionary Self and its addiction to thinking, a beautifully gentle stillness emerges. The way it manifests through you will have its own unique flavour, but it will have a truth and a reality that is breath-taking. Life is allowed to flow through you, expressing itself freely rather than being bound by the distorted perception of your illusionary Self, its associated story and all your accompanying personal baggage.

Initially, when you start practicing *I transcend this* you may find it difficult to separate out your Strategic mind from your Story mind – your thoughts will come too fast to catch hold of and your frustration may build as you feel like a dog chasing its own tail. Over-thinking is the egoic minds way of dragging you back into suffering. It has invested too much time and energy building and sustaining the illusionary Self to let it go without a fight. In this situation take hold of one of these thoughts – for example: 'this method is just a mind game getting me nowhere' and apply *I transcend this* to that thought also. Persevering with *I transcend this* will negate the egoic mind at every turn, reducing your current mind chatter and expose convoluted and muddled thoughts as irrelevant. It cuts right to the core of the problem allowing you to notice potentially stressful and anxious thoughts before they become your reality and so what seemed important and very real, suddenly becomes unimportant and unreal.

Through a simple shift in attention, the thought dissolves and you are left with the space the thought occupied, which asks nothing of you because it does not recognise you. You simply rest in present awareness and life unfolds naturally. The more you practice the easier it will become to drop into present awareness, and as your practice develops and your attention sharpens you will come to a point where it requires more effort to sustain your story than to drop it. You will find yourself spending more time in present moment awareness and start to feel alive again. However, practicing this method is very hard at the beginning because you are attempting to undo a lifetime of conditioning; you will realise how difficult it is when you try holding present moment awareness for more than just a few seconds – the mind pours into silence like the previous Chapter's marbles analogy backfilling the space you are trying to create.

Your reality is the eternal background clarity of the sky, not the temporal clouds of thought floating across it. Your reality resides in the Absolute, not in the illusion of the Self and the insanity of believing the thoughts that feed it. Once you stop identifying with the Self and its ego-drama and notice your thoughts rather than becoming them, you will see with clarity. From that clear space, anything is possible.

9
EGO

Ego is the immediate dictate of human consciousness.

MAX PLANCK

Man lives measuring, and he's the measure of nothing. Not even of himself.

ANTONIO PORCHIA

In previous chapters I have mentioned the ego or more specifically the egoic mind, but what do we mean by ego? Ego is usually associated with certain feelings and behaviours: the gut response rising from the pit of the stomach when we feel belittled; the narcissistic face of personal ambition where the ends justify the means; the envy felt when someone is perceived to be more talented or more popular; or the jealousy felt when we want what someone else has. In the business world, egotism is often equated with self-assertion, where taking what you want and defending it against others is viewed as not only a survival instinct but also a vital ingredient to success, indeed capitalist societies are often portrayed in this dog eat dog fashion (It is worth mentioning here that the structure of western society is more a function of pursuing meaningful endeavour through mutually beneficial interactions than a dominance hierarchy based upon power and greed).

Most of us associate certain negative emotions with the ego, which is then regarded as something to conquer and rise above, or at the very least to control and keep in check. In a spiritual context, the goal is often to drop the ego, thereby attaining the so-called egoless state. However, within the context of this book the ego is not simply one aspect of the Self that gives rise to negative emotions when we are feeling threatened or demeaned, it resides just as much in quiet solitary moments as it does in assertive or defensive moments.

The story we have been taught goes like this: We are thinking, feeling beings with a wealth of emotions, some of which we welcome and others we denounce. Our self-concept (the 'I' or 'me') is a complex set of beliefs that form an image we have of ourselves, one that is predominantly influenced by key people in our life. Most people identify strongly with these core values and beliefs, which affect their behaviour and their outlook on life; although they may not be overtly aware, they are a driving factor in their lives. A person's self-concept might range from high self-worth and self-importance to low self-esteem and a lack of confidence. Our self-concept determines our emotional responses; anger, bitterness, jealousy and envy, can arise in response to certain situations and people. We are sometimes overwhelmed by these powerful emotions and in the aftermath of what we judge as unwelcome emotional reactions, we often make excuses such as *'Sorry, I don't know what came over me. Apologies, I'm not quite myself today. Just give me a moment to pull myself together. Sorry, that was so unlike me. Please forgive me; I just lost it'*. And for every public apology, there are countless internal excuses we make to ourselves. However, such sentiments appear to be a disassociation from certain feelings in an attempt to excuse the resultant behaviour.

These unwanted feelings expose the difficulty of staying in control, and highlight the ephemeral nature of what is believed to be a real and fixed core Self. The ego is a handy scapegoat for such outbursts, but even when we do not recognise it in ourselves, we are quick to label the egotistical behaviour in others. We struggle to control these emotions and to recover our balance afterwards because the idea of a controlling, independent and objective core Self is a fallacy. We have a notion of a solid, fixed and stable centre to our being – an overseer; something that is occasionally so overcome by external events it loses perspective and falls into a whirl of undesirable emotions and actions. There is an urge to separate these negative emotions from what is thought to be our true Self – we miss the fact they arise out of the same illusionary Self and its story of 'me'.

Because most of us have been taught an idealistic Self we need a scapegoat for these aberrations and therefore, in addition to blaming others, we often pin our failings on the ego. There are many theories regarding the ego, a prevalent one is that the negative emotions arising when we are provoked, or the tendency to seek pleasure regardless of the cost, highlight our instinctual animal nature, which is reactive and driven by blind unconscious needs – described by Freud as 'das Es': the IT (*Latin translation: the Id*). Therefore, the story goes, we need to be vigilant at all times – these selfish pleasure seeking desires need to be overcome by adopting a higher moral conscience and practicing benevolence and forgiveness – Freud's 'Das uber-Ich': the over-I (*Latin translation: super-ego*). Freud suggests that most people live between these extremes, mediating between the two in an attempt to live a good/virtuous life while trying to satisfy their strong instinctual drives in a way that is acceptable and palatable – 'Das Ich': the I (*Latin translation: ego*). Depending upon the individual's susceptibilities and their environment, these ideas can be further embellished within a religious or cultural context.

Leaving aside Freud's tripartite theory of personality and the unfortunate Latinised English translation of 'Das Ich' as 'the ego', usually ego refers to what we consider as the objectionable facets of our nature. We divide our behaviours into good and bad, judging whether they are acceptable or unacceptable, welcome or unwelcome, selfless or selfish, egoless or egotistical. We may give in to egotistical behaviour, hoping we can live with the consequences, we may openly welcome the ego and enjoy its fruits, or we may vigilantly attempt to control it and the resultant behaviour, berating ourselves each time it rears its ugly head. However, we are simply tinkering around within an illusion making decisions about which illusionary aspects of ourselves are acceptable and which are not – decisions that are often subconscious scripts created in childhood and the society into which we are born. No two people's self-concepts are the same; everyone has a unique story with their own ethics and morals; we become that story and live it as a reality and when our thoughts and actions do not fit with our story we need to assign blame.

The illusionary Self is conditioned to continually search for emotional experiences, whether arduous or joyous, because the repetitive responses and accompanying thoughts provide the energy it needs to sustain its own pretence. Unfortunately, for many people negative thoughts and the resulting emotions become their reality. Strong attachment to its story is critical to the survival of the Self; therefore, it perpetually wallows in emotional turmoil to maintain its own permanency. Starved of this self-validating feedback loop of negative emotional responses over a long period, the illusionary Self will diminish and may even die. The method of questioning your thoughts with *I transcend this* is an attempt to break that feedback loop.

Once the Self dissolves back into the Absolute the impulses and emotive reactions associated with the ego fall away because there is no individual left and therefore nothing for the unconscious drives to attach to. There is no wasted effort trying to differentiate between all the different versions of your Self and the insanity of trying to work out which version is 'you', in other words the addiction to overthinking and all the associated mind games come to an end. With no investment in the emotions and no back-story to fuel their intensity, your experiences have their moment and then fade away. The experience, whether joy or sadness, pleasure or pain, has a purity and intensity that lasts only its natural duration, *which in reality is very short*, and then disappear because there is no longer a hook into the individual and therefore they cannot be lived as part of the personal story. If everyone could see through their story we would all live in *the I before I am* and there would be peace on earth.

10
MEET ME THERE

Truth is not something outside to be discovered, it is something inside to be realised.

OSHO

To find the origin, trace back the manifestations.

TAO TE CHING

MEET ME THERE

There is a room I would like you to visit. Imagine you are standing in front of a white wooden panelled door. In a moment I will invite you to open it and step through. However, before you enter I ask that you leave some things behind. I ask that you leave your name, your age, your gender, your profession, and your relationship to others. Also, leave your memories, your preferences and every idea and concept you have of yourself, of others and of the world. Leave all your hopes, your fears and your pain along with all your desires and beliefs, and all your questions and accumulated knowledge. Do not worry – they will all be waiting for you exactly as you left them when you return, like a neatly folded pile of clothes. Only when you have relinquished all these things will the door open. I will wait as you place them, one at a time, at your feet.

The door opens and you step inside. The room is large, airy and warm with wooden bleached white walls and floor and a pitched beamed ceiling. There is a faint smell of sandalwood in the air; the room is silent apart from crackling logs and the dancing flames from a wood burner. As the door closes behind you daylight streams in through large floor-to-ceiling windows on the adjacent wall, the rays highlighting fine partials suspended in the air. Through the windows are blue skies with cotton wool clouds floating above green rolling hills. In the centre of the room on a large white rug stands a wooden table and an inviting wingback armchair. On the table is a lit candle. I ask that you sit in the chair and focus on the naked flame. As you sink into the comfortable armchair and gaze at the candle there are no thoughts, just the naked flame and the gentle pops and crackles from the fire, its heat warming your body to the core. I will now ask some questions. As I ask them, be vigilant against any of the things you left at the door creeping back into your consciousness:

Despite leaving your entire identity at the door, is there awareness?
Does this awareness require any effort?
Does this awareness dependent upon anything?
Are the things outside the door secondary to this awareness?
Does this awareness need adding to?
Is there anything closer than this awareness?
Can you be other than this awareness?

Now some statements:

Despite leaving your entire identity at the door, there is awareness.
This awareness requires no effort.
This awareness does not depend upon anything.
The things outside the door are secondary to this awareness.
Nothing needs adding to this awareness.
There is nothing closer than this awareness.
… You are this awareness.

Now blow out the candle. Watch, as the blackened wick releases a spiral of smoke and the pungent burning smell fills your senses. Just as the smoke disperses into the room so the whole room fills your senses. Every detail of your surroundings comes into sharp focus; you see the grains and knots in the wood panelled walls and floorboards and each brushstroke of paint covering them, and every fibre of the soft white rug under your feet and every speck of dust suspended in the sunlight streaming in through the windows. Gazing out you can almost touch the blueness of the sky and feel each blade of grass in the fields below. The heat from the fire warms your skin and you sense the waves radiating deep into your body.

You feel yourself sinking deeper into the armchair, your arms and legs resting heavily on the padded fabric; the chair supports the weight of your whole body perfectly. The warmth of the room matches the warmth of your body as the distinction between you and your surroundings fades and the perceived and perceiver merge. There is no separation and no distance – just abiding stillness. Time vanishes, there is no before and after, and nowhere else to be; nothing needs adding and there is nothing to change, nothing to achieve, no concerns and no desires – just the indescribable beauty of this present moment. Surrendering to this simplicity, free from all attachments, you are truly at rest. For the first time since a baby in the womb you are at peace. You have come home to the place you never left, and now see it for the first time. The Self you were trying to improve and perfect is recognised as an illusion – the perfect being is purged by the perfection of being.

❈

As the smoke from the candle disperses and the burning smell fades, the door opens and, with some reluctance, you stand and leave the room. The door closes behind you and as you gather up your belongings, dressing in the clothes of your identity, you realise they are only relatively important. Those things that felt comfortable before still feel comfortable, and those that were uncomfortable are still uncomfortable, however, regardless of how they fit, you realise they are not you; you are the untouched stillness beyond form – the pure awareness within.

This room is always available, you can enter whenever you wish; simply drop your attachments and the door will open.

11
TIME

What then is time? If no one asks me, I know what it is. If I wish to explain it to him who asks, I do not know.

SAINT AUGUSTINE

The intuitive recognition of the instant, thus reality... is the highest act of wisdom.

D. T. SUZUKI

I am sure we are all familiar with the following phrases: 'If only I had the time – there just aren't enough hours in the day – it's not the right time – where did the time go – I wish things would slow down – I'm running out of time – if I had my time over again'. You could argue that one of the biggest constraining factors and stresses in our lives is our relationship with time, specifically the idea that we have a finite amount of it and must therefore make the most of the time we have been given, or the time we have left. There are often deadlines we have to meet and future events we need to plan for, both of which impinge on our available time and can affect our current wellbeing.

So what exactly is time? We may think of it in many ways: as the ticking clock, the ageing process, the changing seasons, as an arrow flying in one direction charting our life stories from birth to death, moving relentlessly into the future and leaving the past in its wake. Time seems as real as the air we breathe; inextricably linked to our lives, it is a dependable touchstone constantly referenced and measured against, often passing so quickly we are chasing it, and sometimes so slow we become bored with time on our hands. But what exactly is the intrinsic nature of time? As the quote from Saint Augustine succinctly expresses, time seems to be such an obvious commodity until we attempt to describe it.

So what is time in and of itself? Events appear to occur in time, but does time exist independent of the events happening within it? In other words, if there were no events and nothing changed, thus leaving nothing to measure, would time exist? Equally, could it exist if there was nothing observing its passage – without sentient beings to conceptualise time, can it have any meaning whatsoever? Do we exist within an objective phenomenon called time, carried along on the crest of an ever-present *now* that flows from the past into the future, or is time a construct of the human mind?

We measure the passage of time in hours, minutes and seconds, and in days, weeks, months and years. Our clocks measure small timescales, and our calendars larger ones, but what exactly are we measuring? Perhaps we are simply quantifying change; does the concept of time have any meaning without it? We watch a candle burn, and we understand change by comparing its present form to its previous, and can then deduce its future form. Those changes we say take time. Our experience shows that the candle changes in one direction; it continues burning down until it is extinguished. Similarly, we believe our lives are burning down in one direction. However, there is only ever the present moment being experienced: the luminosity of the naked flame, and both the past and the future are defined by this present moment. The concept of change and its measurement are completely dependent upon the present moment, so perhaps understanding the present is the key to understanding time.

We have talked about the present in previous chapters and of not allowing the story of our past or our hopes for the future to take us away from this present moment of being-ness. The phrase *I transcend this* is an attempt to reconnect with the present moment by noticing that our thoughts are taking us away from it. In terms of time then, what exactly is the present moment? Can we measure it? Does it have duration? Does it exist for a second, half a second, or one hundredth of a second? Is it possible to measure it in time, or is it a fleeting temporal perception that only has meaning when experienced through a sentient being? If the present moment can only be comprehended in terms of a subjective conscious awareness and cannot be objectively measured, then can it actually exist within a timeframe? Furthermore, how can we isolate the present from the immediate future and from the immediate past when it seems indistinguishable from both? At what point does the present moment become the immediate past, and at what point does the immediate future become the present moment? It would appear that the demarcation between the present and the past, and between the present and the future, is impossible to define. We do not seem to be able to draw a line in the sand, prior to which is the past and after which is the future. So all we appear to be left with is that subjective temporal experience out of which we create a before and an after, a past and a future. If the present cannot be measured in time then perhaps it is timeless?

The suggestion that time is subjective, and therefore relative to the observer is borne out by physics, which has established that time has no independent objective reality: it does not exist as a universal constant but is always relative to the observer. In 1902 a technical assistant in a Swiss patent office began a series of thought experiments that would lead to the now famous Special Theory of Relativity (later to be reworked as his General Theory of Relativity). Albert Einstein ushered in the 20th century with two assumptions: firstly, his principle of relativity stating that all motion is relative to other observable objects, and that there is no such thing as absolute rest; and secondly, the speed of light is constant, having the same value, 'c', with respect to any observer either at rest or moving uniformly. This led to the mind-bending conclusion that in order for all observers to measure the same value for the speed of light, time would have to flow differently for different observers. Einstein showed that time and space were relative, and the passage of time was dependent upon the speed of the observer, so the faster one travelled, the slower time passed in relation to someone who was stationary. In short, moving clocks ticked at a slower rate.

However, in our everyday life because we are all moving at roughly the same speed, all measurements of time are *virtually* identical – virtually. Most speeds are far too slow to produce observable differences, but small variations in time have been measured at higher speeds. The Hafele and Keating Experiment in 1971 (Hafele J. C. & Keating R. E., 1972) placed atomic clocks upon commercial jets and flew them twice around the world, and then compared the clocks against others on the ground. The results did show differences in time but they were measured not in minutes or even seconds but in nanoseconds (a thousand millionths of a second). To give an idea of how small these differences are, one nanosecond is to one second what one second is to thirty years. The speeds necessary to produce differences measured in days, months or years are far greater than any speeds we can travel using current technology, and such velocities would need to be approaching the speed of light at 186,000 miles per second. And again, to put that in context, an object travelling at such a speed would circle the earth's equator seven times per second.

Although we cannot travel anywhere near such speeds, physicists are able to study particle collisions that routinely reach 99.9% of the speed of light, using massive machines called particle accelerators (electrified hollow evacuated tubes through which charged particles are accelerated). From an external observer's viewpoint, the inner clock of such a travelling particle runs much slower than a particle at rest by a factor that is in precise agreement with special relativity. However, back in our everyday world, where such immense speeds play no part, time passes at the same rate for everyone. Of course, subjectively speaking, we experience big psychological variations depending upon our situation. So, for instance, five minutes spent reading a captivating novel appears to go far quicker than five minutes waiting on hold during a stressful phone call. Superficially at least, the rate at which time (subjectively) passes, seems to depend upon our level of engagement and enjoyment in the moment.

Relativistic, philosophical and psychological contemplations aside, there is no escaping the fact that on a practical level the functioning of society is dependent upon a shared understanding and measurement of time. It was during the mid-1800s that the railways of Great Britain adopted Greenwich Mean Time (GMT) as a standard time across the island. Then soon after the United States and Canadian railroads set standard time zones across the continent. Prior to such standardisation, time had been a local matter for each individual town or city – one can only imagine the problems that created for those travelling great distances. In today's world, we accept a standard time as a fact of life, giving little thought to its arbitrary and contrived history. All daily routines are run against this standard, which controls virtually all areas of our lives, and on a larger scale, there is a timeline upon which we measure progress through life. We believe we are on a one-way journey travelling from birth to death. Our current location on this timeline is identified by the number of years since birth, but as mentioned, there is also an ever-present subjective position in time: the conscious awareness of the present moment – *now*. Practically speaking, this is defined by measuring against standard time, for example: it is now 11:54 am on a Monday morning. This practical description of now can provide useful information, such as there are only six minutes until the midday news, but in a wider context, it is a reference point that draws upon a vast personal history, and sets up short-term plans and longer-term goals. And, of course, plans and goals are a reminder of the limited time we have in this world. If there is any doubt that time's arrow flows in one direction, we only need look in the mirror and witness the ageing process – we are growing older not younger. Such change is methodically measured by clocks ticking off seconds, minutes and hours, and by calendars relentlessly turning over days, weeks, months and years.

Removed from society's artificial demarcations, nature appears to have its own cycles, as evidenced by the changing seasons and the sun's daily arc across the sky. For prehistoric man, these celestial observations and the changing seasons informed nomadic movements and farming rotations, and marked sacred festivals. In these earlier eras, there were certainly predictable events, but time was not a fixed digital regulator imposed upon life; rather, it was a two-way analogue interaction with nature. In today's digital age, agreeing upon a shared standard time is necessary in order to regulate, organise and synchronise our modern lives; it is vital in maintaining social coherence and order, but in the move from analogue to digital perhaps we have lost something in translation. Within the context of our modern era, time is essentially a social convenience; but what of its intrinsic nature, its objective qualities and the apparent transience of the present moment?

Perhaps our relationship to the present moment can unlock the riddle of time. Could it be that time is only meaningful to the human mind – that time is a concept relying upon the conscious awareness of change, and that outside of the conditioned mind it is meaningless? The Absolute – *the I before I am* – lives within the eternal present and the eternal present within it. Out of this unchanging eternal source the illusionary Self spins out a past and projects a future, a before and after, creating time through subjective experience. This conscious experience of time is part of the illusion of being a finite limited form. Once freed from that illusion it becomes apparent that we are not moving through time from the past into the future and time does not *flow*, nor are we carried within it; but that we are only ever in the eternal present moment.

However, our subjective 'I am' experience suggests otherwise. Our minds are conditioned to think linearly and sequentially and so rather than being in the eternal present, we feel more like passengers on a train travelling from the past into the future, the stations along the way serving as markers on our journey. Our departure from the last station is given a time in the past, and arrival at the next is given a time in the future. The distances between stations are measured in various ways: days, weeks, months, years and decades. The stations are sometimes milestone events, such as birthdays, anniversaries, religious festivals or the passing of loved ones, but are often as mundane as *last Tuesday or tomorrow afternoon*. However, as mentioned, there is a fixed and immovable source existing beneath the subjective experience of the present moment and therefore in all the past and future 'stations' of our lives. That source – *the I before I am* – is the track upon which the train is travelling. The track is the Absolute – an immovable unchanging constant holding every present moment and all past and future ones. It has no departure or arrival, no before or after, no past or future, because it is the departure and the arrival, the before and the after, the past and the future. It does not redefine our understanding of time; instead, it negates it, because if all stations are One, there can be no movement between them, and with no movement, there is no time.

At a deeper level of consciousness, we are not passengers on a train moving through time from the past into the future; we are the unmoved eternal Absolute – the track that holds all. The track lying at the station of our birth is the same track that lies at the station of our first day at school, which is the same track that lies at the station of our 18th birthday, and at our final birthday and our last breath. The same track lies under all our history, right up to this present moment and extends to every so-called 'future' event. This track is the present moment – the only place we can ever be.

Unmoved and untouched by the apparent rush of life's train, and all the subjective experiences therein, the Absolute quietly sits, the ground of all being, joining all pasts and all futures, holding the entire cacophony of life within the eternal present. The illusionary Self cannot survive in the present moment; it lives in a story of past and future, carrying the dead weight of a fixed past and projecting that solidified rock into an imaginary future. Once the illusionary Self and its limiting story is exposed, life bursts forth and every moment is lived in the freedom of present awareness. You become fully awake in every action where nothing you do is a means to an end – you are no longer the story of the burning candle, you become the luminosity of the naked flame. *'When you do something, you should burn yourself up completely, like a good bonfire, leaving no trace of yourself'* (Shunryu Suzuki).

As a child building sandcastles on the beach or riding your bicycle you lived in the eternal present effortlessly. As a manifestation of the Absolute, you taste the beauty and simplicity of life once more. You return to *the I before I am*; building sandcastles – filling your bucket with wet sand, you are fully present in the action, your senses filled with the salty sea air, the sound of seagulls and waves breaking on the shore as the sun warms you to the core. And this presence can be experienced anywhere, you do not need idyllic conditions such as a magnificent sunset or a walk in nature or a sandy beach. It is always available, it can be experienced whilst washing your hands or waiting in line at the checkout or walking down a busy high street. Just like a child building sandcastles on the beach, everything you do lives in the present moment – the action and the awareness become one as doing and being merge into timeless presence.

12

INNER REALMS

*Anyone who is not shocked by quantum theory
has not understood it*

NIELS BOHR

*Observations not only disturb what is to be
measured, they produce it.*

PASCUAL JORDAN

In the previous chapter I questioned whether time exists as an objective reality – that is to say, whether it is an appearance in the mind, rather than a phenomena existing outside of our perceptions and conceptualisations. (Indeed one can question the 'reality' and the nature of all objects outside of our phenomenological perceptions of them). I suggested that the flow of time appears to arise through our subjective conscious awareness, but that at a deeper level of consciousness – *the I before I am*, the present moment is in fact timeless.

I would now like to turn our attention to the inner realm of the physical world and see whether there is an underlying objective reality at the deepest and most fundamental level. To do this, we will take a trip together into the microscopic world of subatomic particles (*particles smaller than or occurring within an atom*). This world behaves very strangely and is described through a branch of physics called quantum mechanics. Do not worry there will be no formulas or equations and no assumptions that you have any understanding of either quantum theory or subatomic particles. Firstly, I will give a brief description of atoms and subatomic particles and then I will show using an experimental analogy just how bizarre that world is and how the conscious observer seems to play a fundamental role. Finally, I will look at both the inner realms of the material and spiritual worlds from an overarching metaphysical perspective.

Everything in the universe that has mass is made of fundamental particles called atoms (apart from dark matter, which I will come to later). Atoms held together by chemical bonds form molecules. A water molecule, for example, consists of two hydrogen atoms and one oxygen atom (H_2O), whereas a vitamin C molecule is made up of six carbon atoms, eight hydrogen atoms and six oxygen atoms ($C_6H_8O_6$) arranged in specific patterns. In addition to molecules, there are elements (a substance made entirely from one type of atom) and compounds (a substance made of two or more elements chemically combined). Basically, everything around us – everything we can see, taste, touch and hear – is reducible to atoms. It was during the late 19th and early 20th centuries that scientists proved the existence of atoms (named from the Greek *atomos* meaning indivisible), but soon after it was found that the mighty atom is not the fundamental and indivisible object they had believed – it is actually made up of smaller particles. They discovered the atom is formed from three basic subatomic particles that are held together by strong nuclear and electromagnetic forces: electrons (carrying a negative electrical charge), protons (carrying a positive electrical charge) and neutrons (carrying no electrical charge).

The protons and neutrons form a nucleus at the centre of the atom around which the electrons travel in orbits or shells, and the protons and neutrons in the nucleus are themselves made of smaller particles called quarks. The proton has two 'up' quarks each with a charge of $+2/3$, and one 'down' quark with a charge of $-1/3$ giving an overall charge of $+1$. The neutron has two 'down' and one 'up' quark giving an overall charge of 0. The number of protons in the atom gives its atomic number and determines its element, so an atom with 79 protons is always gold, whereas an atom with 8 protons is always oxygen. The electrons orbit the atom in different layers or shells, and atoms are grouped by the number of electrons in their outer shell (the orbit furthest from the nucleus). This outer shell is called the valence shell and the electrons in it are called valence electrons. It is these electrons that are transferred and shared allowing atoms to gain, lose or share electrons in chemical reactions leading to bonding. In this way, the two hydrogen atoms can bond with a single oxygen atom to give H_2O.

Each atom, although infinitesimally small, is found to be 99.9 % empty space. Therefore, if the nucleus was scaled up to the size of a pea, the orbiting electrons would be half a mile away and circling a circumference of just over 3 miles. Since all matter is made of atoms, the universe we can see and measure is more than 99.9% empty. Moreover, there is even less substance to hold on to because this normal matter makes up only 4% of the universe – the rest is made of 'stuff' that cannot as yet be detected or comprehended called dark energy and dark matter. Astronomers and physicists are trying to find out what dark energy and dark matter are, as their existence is only inferred by other observations, such as the accelerating expansion of the universe and certain gravitational effects. So in effect, we do not remotely understand 96 % of the universe, and all our understanding and laws of physics fall into the remaining 4%.

This model of subatomic particles, consisting of a nucleus with orbiting electrons, replaced the model of a universe made of solid indivisible spherical atoms that obey the classical physics of larger objects, such as billiard balls. While this model gave a new understanding of the atom, the behaviour of these subatomic particles was found to be very strange to say the least. Due to the German physicist Werner Heisenberg's Uncertainty Principle, it became apparent that it was not possible to accurately describe or measure what was happening at this subatomic level (the particles inside the atom). It turns out that a particle's position and momentum (a property related to speed or velocity) cannot be measured simultaneously; the more accurately we know its position, the less certain we are about its momentum and vice versa – importantly, this was not a limitation of the measuring equipment but an intrinsic limitation of the subatomic world.

However, this model of electrons moving in shells or orbits around a central nucleus was not the full picture. It appeared that electrons did not in fact travel around the nucleus but were a 'wave' entirely surrounding the nucleus, and that their exact position and momentum could not be measured at any given instant. This new understanding gave the electrons the properties of both a particle and a wave, making descriptions inexact and conceptual models difficult to imagine. The electron could be in two places at the same time, and could travel simultaneously from point A to point B along all possible paths. It was also found that the electron jumps in and out of existence, appearing more often at the crest of a wave pattern; therefore, the wave was in effect a map of the particle's position over time.

It fell to Erwin Schrodinger to describe this behaviour through his wave functions. Despite the difficulty imagining electrons as waves, Schrodinger gave a precise mathematical model, not only for the distribution of electrons within the atom, but for the behaviour and motion of particles across the entire universe. In this understanding, the quantum mechanical atom consists of a nucleus surrounded by clouds that represent the electrons. For example, the single electron in the hydrogen atom is spread across all possible locations within the atom, and its allowed orbit is the exact point at which the probability of an electron appearing reaches its maximum. In other words, the shells or orbits of the electrons are the places where the probability of finding an electron is the greatest, based upon Schrodinger's wave functions. The electron no longer exists as a single discrete particle that follows specific orbits, but is a wave of probability forming a cloud surrounding the nucleus. This is not a very satisfactory conceptual model in terms of being easy to imagine, but nonetheless it describes what is happening at the subatomic level.

As if this quantum mechanical world was not strange enough, physicists found that they could no longer separate themselves from the phenomena they were observing, because the act of measuring affected the results. An experiment at this subatomic level produced contradictory results depending upon how the physicist chose to observe it. If measured a certain way, they would see a particular result, and if measured a different way, they would see a different result. Therefore, with no change to the experiment's initial conditions, the results differed depending upon the method of measurement. When working at the quantum level, the idea of an independent observer conducting experiments that produced consistent objective results had to be re-thought. Physicists found they were part of (or entangled with) the experiment, and far from being objective spectators, it appeared they were inextricably linked to the subatomic particles being measured. By simply observing, they were affecting the particle's behaviour. The following analogy shows how bizarre such behaviour would appear if it were possible to scale up a quantum-level experiment to the macro level of our everyday world.

❦

For this analogy of a scaled up quantum-level experiment I would like you to imagine an apparatus consisting of flexible hollow plastic tubing and dozens of white marbles. The tubing is opaque black with an internal diameter just wide enough for the marbles to roll through. The apparatus begins with an open-ended straight section of tubing which then branches in two. Each branch forms two opposing semi-circles that join back together, and where they re-join there is a final straight section that finishes with an open end. The whole structure is lying on a wooden board angled on a slight downward slope. Marbles placed in the top end of the tube will roll down the first straight section, and then take either the left or the right branch, run through the semi-circular section, join back with the final straight section and then exit from the open end. There is a large bowl positioned under the exit to collect the marbles.

The whole design is such that the marbles placed in the open-ended starting section of the tube have a 50/50 chance of rolling down either the left or right semi-circular branch before exiting down the final straight section. Because the tube is opaque, we cannot see the path of the marbles, and so there is no way of knowing whether they will take the left or the right branch. All we observe is the marbles entering the top straight section of the tube, and then moments later, exiting one by one from the bottom straight section into the bowl. Now let us add another element to this experiment. Halfway down the left semi-circular branch of the tube we insert a small nozzle that, when turned on, sprays a continuous fine mist of blue paint into the tube, and similarly halfway down the right semi-circular branch of the tube, we insert another small nozzle that, when turned on, sprays a continuous fine mist of yellow paint. (Assume for the purposes of this analogy that the sprays of blue and yellow paint remain in each respective branch and do not mix further down the tubing). The final piece to the apparatus is a hinged flap located inside the top straight section of the tube at the point where it branches in two. Using an external lever, this flap has three settings: it can close off the left branch, it can close off the right branch, or it can open both branches.

Now let us begin our experiment. Firstly, using the lever we close off the left branch of the tube so that the only path available to the marbles is the right branch through the yellow spray. We turn on both paint sprays and then insert a funnel into the open end of the top section of the tube allowing us to pour in dozens of white marbles. What we observe at the end of the apparatus are newly painted yellow marbles filling the bowl as they exit one by one from the bottom tube. No surprise there. Next, we turn off the sprays, empty the bowl, clean the apparatus and repeat the experiment, but this time we set the lever to close off the right branch of the tube, so now the only path available is the left branch through the blue spray. Again, we turn on both sprays and pour in dozens of white marbles. This time, as we would expect, the bowl fills with dozens of newly painted blue marbles.

For the next experiment, we again turn off the sprays, empty the bowl and clean the apparatus, but this time we set the lever to open both branches, and once again turn on the sprays and pour in dozens of white marbles. The marbles now have a 50/50 chance of taking either the left or the right branch, and so we would expect the bowl to fill with roughly equal amounts of newly painted blue and yellow marbles – the sprayed colour depending upon which path each marble has taken. We watch as the bowl starts filling with newly painted marbles, but they are not blue or yellow – they are all green! For all the marbles collecting in the bowl to be green, each individual one would have had to pass through the blue and yellow spray at the same time; in other words, each individual marble would have had to pass through both branches of the tube simultaneously!

This is clearly nonsense, so to investigate further, rather than sending a constant stream of marbles down the tube, we decide to simplify the experiment and send down just one at a time. So we repeat the experiment. Once we have reset the apparatus, cleaned the tubing and turned on the sprays, we close off the left branch and place a single white marble into the top tube. As we would expect, it exits from the bottom tube collecting in the bowl and is painted yellow. Resetting the apparatus, we then close off the right branch, and again place a single white marble into the top tube. As expected, it exits from the bottom tube collecting in the bowl, and is painted blue. Now for the big test: After resetting and cleaning again, we open up both branches of the tube, turn on the sprays and place a single white marble into the top tube. Moments later, it exits from the bottom tube, collecting in the bowl and is painted green! In disbelief, we place another white marble into the top tube, and it too collects in the bowl and is painted green. We continue placing single white marbles into the top tube, and each time they exit painted green. This appears to confirm the mind-bending results of our first experiment – the single marble must somehow be passing through both branches of the tube, which is clearly impossible.

Following much head scratching, we decide this bizarre behaviour needs further investigation, as the results seem to be breaking physical laws not to mention defying our common sense! We need to see which branch the single marble actually takes because clearly it cannot be taking both. We need to see what is happening inside the tube after it branches in two. So we cut a small opening into the tube at the point just after it branches to the left, and an identical opening at the point just after it branches to the right. These *apertures* give us a view inside both branches of the tube without affecting the marble's movement, so now as the marble rolls past either aperture we will see it and therefore know the path it has taken. This should give us a clearer picture of what is going on.

We empty and clean the apparatus once again, start the sprays and set the lever to open both branches and place a single white marble in the top tube. This time we observe it as it rolls past the aperture in the left branch, subsequently exits from the bottom tube, collects in the bowl and is painted blue. No surprise. We continue to place white marbles in the top and observe which branch each one takes. Because it is a 50/50 chance, we observe through the apertures some marbles taking the left branch and others the right, and the bowl gradually fills with blue and yellow painted marbles respectively. This is exactly the behaviour we would expect. The apparatus is identical to our previous experiment, apart from the fact that we can now observe through the apertures which branch each marble takes inside the tube – we now know its location. So we perform one final experiment. We cover up both apertures with black tape so that we can no longer see inside either branch of the tube. We then reset the apparatus and with both branches open, we repeat the last experiment, placing a single white marble in the top tube. It exits from the bottom tube collecting in the bowl and is painted green! We continue placing white marbles in the top tube, they begin collecting in the bowl and each and every one is painted green.

Repeating this experiment day after day, week after week, month after month will give the same results: with both branches open and no observation apertures, each marble will exit from the bottom tube, collect in the bowl and be painted green. If we open the apertures and observe the marble's path, it will collect in the bowl and be painted either blue or yellow, corresponding to the branch we have observed it taking. Both experiments are identical apart from in one we are observing the marble's path and in the other we are not. This clearly makes no sense; however, these results mirror the behaviour of particles being observed by physicists at the subatomic level.

In the equivalent actual quantum experiment, when making its journey, the subatomic particle (the marble) is said to be in a state of quantum superposition. Which means it is in all possible states simultaneously (passing through both left and right branches at the same time) until it is observed or measured for a specific result (observing it through the aperture), whereupon it appears in only one location (left branch or right branch). Another way quantum physicists describe this behaviour is that prior to being measured (or observed), the particle has no specific location but is a probability wave of potentialities spread out over all possible locations, and that the act of measuring (or observing) collapses the wave function to one location.

I am sure you will agree that this behaviour is baffling and defies all logic. Returning to my experimental analogy and describing it in quantum terms, prior to observing through the open apertures, each marble's path is said to be in a state of superposition appearing to pass through both branches simultaneously (collecting in the bowl and painted green). By observing its path (measuring for a specific result), the superposition of states collapses, and the marble collects in the bowl and is painted the colour corresponding to the branch we observed it taking: the left branch (blue) or right branch (yellow). Our observation collapses the wave function. Or if you prefer, the subatomic world is in a suspended state of indeterminacy, until it is observed or measured whereupon a concrete reality results.

(*The above analogy is based upon Thomas Young's famous double-slit experiment where matter and energy can display the characteristics of either a wave or a particle, depending upon how they are observed. In my analogy, the green-painted marbles represent the interference pattern built up gradually on the photographic plate, indicating that each individual particle must somehow pass through both slits*).

❊

When looking deep into the fabric of the universe in search of its fundamental properties, we uncover a subatomic world that can only be described in terms of probabilities, within which the behaviour of its particles are all but incomprehensible. This subatomic world upon which everything we experience is built is inexplicable even to the quantum physicists, most of whom restrict themselves to a purely mathematical understanding. Quantum physics accurately describes this subatomic world but not without demolishing the central tenets of classical physics, and assaulting our common sense in the process. The building blocks of matter turn out not to be blocks at all, but rather clouds of probabilities, possibilities and potentialities in a constant state of fluidity – a place where particles wink in and out of existence, and where our classical understanding of space, time and motion can play no part.

The energy vibrating at the heart of every atom in the universe, the very fabric of everything around us, including our own bodies, is playing by its own rules – rules that fly in the face of how we experience the world. However, despite the incomprehensible behaviour exhibited in this subatomic world, it is mathematically consistent: the predictions arising from quantum theory have been proven time and again to have a precision far beyond anything classical physics can match. Quantum theory has brought countless technological advances: the laser, the electron microscope, Magnetic Resonance Imaging (MRI), and the transistor – the heart of every circuit board in every computer. Nevertheless, attempting to investigate this subatomic world introduces the observer problem. It would appear that the consciousness of the observer not only affects the outcome, it actually creates it. This questions the objectivity of the external observer, and in turn questions the whole experimental process because it appears that consciousness precedes phenomena. In other words, consciousness is not a secondary phenomenon or by-product of the brain, but gives rise to all phenomena: that it is the starting point from which everything arises. In this model, rather than an objective world of phenomena lying in wait for a conscious being to perceive it, consciousness comes first and all phenomena arise out of it. Consciousness before manifestation – *the I before I am*.

This metaphysical notion of a universal consciousness could explain another quantum phenomenon known as non-locality or entanglement, whereby particles starting out as a connected pair and then subsequently separated by large distances, can instantaneously know each other's state. This empirically verifiable fact breaks Einstein's law that nothing travels faster than the speed of light. Furthermore, if we take the prevalent model of the universe as beginning with a singularity followed by the Big Bang, then billions of years later everything in this expanding universe would still be entangled. Everything would be connected to everything else, a single fundamental reality weaved into the very fabric of the universe connecting everything – not via signals that depend upon time and space, but a connection that's instantaneous and unmediated. Time and space connected by a single underlying Absolute.

Deep underlying realities can have far-reaching effects regardless of whether they are describable in ways that make sense. Looking deep within the Self will lead to some rather strange conclusions that seem to have little relevance to everyday life. Similarly, trying to understand the subatomic world is incredibly difficult, the harder scientists try to uncover an objective reality, the less certain that reality appears – it would seem that the underlying reality of the physical world is not a thing that can be measured or dissected into comprehendible fundamental parts. To borrow a quantum phrase: reality is a superposition of all possible states. The illusionary Self could be described as the collapse of that superposition into each of our subjective realities. Questioning that reality is difficult, but if one turns inwards and observes this illusionary Self, then the incomprehensible underlying Absolute will seep in little by little until a tipping point is reached. Such a tipping point will flip your reality in a sudden and irreversible paradigm shift as the isolated constricted Self dissipates back to its source, or to phrase it differently: the collapsed superposition of your individual reality merges with the nebulous indeterminate cloud of the Absolute and you awake to *the I before I am*.

The search for an underlying substance or reality to the Self, and the search for an underlying substance or reality to the universe, both fail to find a comprehensible and indivisible source. In the material world, the idea that physical reality can be reduced to objective spherical atoms obeying the classical laws of physics has long gone. The deeper science looks into the material universe, the less objective substance it finds, until at the subatomic level physical reality is reduced to fuzzy clouds of probabilities and empty space. There are no solid building blocks from which the world is made, similarly, there is no solid individual Self at the centre of your being; any discernible underlying properties appear vague and incomprehensible to the intellect.

In everyday life, our conventional understanding of who and what we are, and our view of the human being as a separate independent entity whose essence is held whole and complete, residing within a physical body makes perfect sense. And because this model seems to work at a superficial level, there is seldom a need to look deeper – just as classical physics went unchallenged for so long because it seemed to describe the physical forces that shaped the world we live in. Those who are prepared to look beyond conventional understandings and accepted ways of thinking, those who turn the spotlight within and recognise their inherent emptiness – they are the 'quantum pioneers' of Self enquiry.

13

YOUR BODY

Heaven and earth and I are of the same root, The ten-thousand things and I are of one substance

SÊNG-CHAO / SŌJŌ

Don't look for God in the sky; look within your own body.

OSHO

I have mentioned before that for the Self to relinquish its stranglehold over your life it has to achieve the near impossible: it must somehow realise its own illusionary nature, and this is where your body may help. It is no coincidence that many meditation practices concentrate on breathing in an attempt to quiet the mind. By focusing on the physical living/breathing entity underpinning all psychological, spiritual and rational thoughts, it can become apparent that the biological organism we call the body is neither a container for the soul nor a puppet for the Self, but an opening through which the Absolute shines.

In the previous chapters we looked at time and the fundamental constituents of matter and found it impossible to pin either down to a fixed objective reality and that both are relative to, or – *in quantum terms* – entangled with, the observer. Quite clearly in these discussions we used concepts, ideas and thought experiments, but the intention was to highlight, at the most fundamental level, all we can work with are mathematical abstractions such as Schrodinger's wave function or Einstein's special relativity formulas and field equations. There appears to be no irreducible independent objective reality. I used the term 'observer' because it suited the idea of an experimenter measuring results, but the observer is another name for a conscious human being. We are all observers but our conscious attention focuses on a narrow band of concepts and ideas we have been taught in an effort to make sense of the world, and through constant identification with those ideas and concepts, we become them. In other words, over the years our *observations* are subjectively filtered through learned conceptual ideas, memories of past experiences and subconscious processes, forming our story – the illusionary Self. We do not see things as they are – we see a reflection of ourselves, and because we use a distorted mirror (the illusionary Self) then our understanding is distorted too. This chapter will look at the body, *which does not distort reality*, and investigate the relationship we have with it – we will look at the connection between our biography and our biology.

From within the stillness of the Absolute, it is realised that the Self is a dream character interacting with other dream characters and dream states, its form dancing with other forms in the play of life. Most people spend their lives within the dream of an illusionary Self; trapped in our thoughts we constantly interpret the world by referencing our story. However, as mentioned previously, even within the dream the deeper consciousness of *the I before I am* can seep in and at certain moments we may sense a vague uneasiness at our core, a feeling that something is fundamentally wrong. This feeling is usually interpreted as something that is missing rather than something being false, and the ensuing attempts to fill the apparent emptiness shapes most people's lives without them realising. There is a constant search for something to satiate this need. For some, the search is a spiritual one to gain inner meaning and greater purpose, for others, acquiring knowledge or possessions are different attempts to fill the same need. Some attempt to satisfy this need by overeating, drinking or taking drugs, which can lead to cravings and habitual patterns, and in many cases compulsions and addictions. Addictions can have many root causes but are often a consequence of trying to fill an emptiness within, where the search for lasting happiness is abandoned in favour of immediate gratification.

When years of acquiring knowledge, experiences and material possessions fail to bring happiness or contentment, we may find ourselves perfunctorily going through the motions of daily life in a somewhat subdued and depressive state, where the only relief seems to be to consume more of the same thereby repeating the cycle of temporary happiness followed by long periods of melancholy. However, while we are feeding the mind and body, and trying to find happiness though spiritual or material means, we miss the fact that it is the physical body that can point to the reality of our situation because it lies outside of the shared illusion. Although the body seems fundamental to our sense of Self, its biology does not recognise the illusionary Self or its story, refusing to be a part of it. I will pick this up again later, but first let us look at how we relate to the body.

So how does the Self view the body – what is our relationship to the body? I suggest that generally we tend to view our bodies mainly in negative ways; they frustrate and even disappoint us, never looking quite how we would like, often letting us down and most annoyingly growing old on us. Over the years we witness a gradual deterioration as the physical pursuits we once enjoyed take more effort and recovery takes longer. Joints and muscles ache more than they used to and agility diminishes as we lose the flexibility we once enjoyed. Wrinkles begin to age our face and deteriorating eyesight may mean glasses. Hearing may be impaired, hair may grey and thin, and we may gain weight as our overall metabolism slows. This decline happens to a body in good health, and is a natural result of ageing; however, if we suffer from poor health then the problems associated with growing old can be exacerbated.

Heart disease and cancer are two of the main killers in Western societies: stress, congenital issues, environmental factors and lifestyles being the main causes. The multitude of other diseases, viruses, genetic and environmental conditions that can adversely affect our bodies are too numerous to mention. The net result is that many of us live with ill health or eventually succumb to it. With all these factors, it is hardly surprising then that our body seems to define us in a limited way: its frailty and mortality becomes our frailty and mortality. Trapped within this mortal frame, and perhaps in retaliation to the apparent hopelessness of our situation, we often abuse the body through the excesses and vices mentioned. This self-destructive behaviour is sometimes an extreme reaction to decay and mortality – often driven by an insatiable need to live every moment and seize every experience, even when it is detrimental to our health. Some give scant attention to the body and neglect or abuse it, they may live a hedonistic life or retreat to the intellectual world of their minds; viewing the body as an instrument for gratification or an annoying inconvenience and treat it accordingly.

The flipside to this destructive and neglectful behaviour is to subject the body to excessive exercise and obsessive health regimes. Attaining a peak of physical fitness gives many a sense of achievement and personal wellbeing, and although not halting the ageing process, may appear to slow it. However, those who define themselves purely through their physical abilities and attainments have a severe readjustment to make when their bodies can no longer match their expectations. Often the quest is for physical perfection where youth and beauty are thought to be the key to happiness, and so energies are focused upon surface appearance. Striving for the 'body beautiful' can take many forms but again, usually involves obsessive exercise and strict dieting. For many, the improvements are too slow or do not meet expectations, and so shortcuts to perfection are sought through supplements, diet pills, performance-enhancing drugs and cosmetic surgery. No pain, no gain is the battle cry as the war against ageing is fought (*and lost*) in gyms and health clubs around the world.

Not surprisingly, the desire to change one's physical appearance is big business, and so companies aggressively market health and fitness products, promising a shortcut to the body beautiful. There are countless products on offer from the latest exercise machines and fitness programmes to diet pills, slimming drinks and anti-ageing creams. Models are paid fortunes to endorse a wide range of products to create a whole fantasy lifestyle that people buy into – ignoring the fact models have their genetics (and airbrushing) to thank for their appearance, not the products they endorse. For many, the body symbolises not simply their physical identity but their whole essence, and they believe keeping it young and making it perfect, keeps them young and makes them perfect. However, striving to achieve these physical goals and trying to sustain them over time is a losing battle.

The aforementioned lifestyles are generalisations based on characteristics we are all familiar with; however, in reality people are far more complex. Our lives are likely to be multi-faceted and probably less extreme; we may lead a more measured and moderate lifestyle. We may be health-conscious to a degree, take regular exercise, and feel reasonably happy with our body image and enjoy good health. Over the years, our interests and goals may vary but not wildly, and although we may overindulge occasionally and have the odd blowout, we are soon back on track. Our way of life depends to a greater or lesser extent upon our environment: our social group, who we live with, where we live and where we work, and as these variables change over time so does our lifestyle. We may feel like a bundle of contradictions to ourselves while appearing to others as fairly stable and centred, and perhaps only a select few get to see the inner turmoil beneath our calm exterior. Irrespective of how we live our life, our own state of health and how we regard our body, we will be aware of illness and infirmity in those we are close to or by simply observing other people in our daily life – sobering reminders that as we age our life will change too. If we give any thought to the stark reality of growing old, we may, quite understandably, have a sense of urgency to enjoy life and live it to the full while we still can – and of course 'living life to the full' plays out differently for everyone.

Within the illusion of the Self we feel inextricably linked to our bodies, in fact we may see them as one and the same. However, as our body ages, and we experience its gradual and inevitable deterioration, such impermanence and decay may conflict with an innate awareness of something that seems immune to the ravages of time. This may be experienced as an unchanging, permanent inner core of our being, whereas the body is something we believe will ultimately fail us. We have all heard or made comments like: *inside I don't feel any different than I did 'nn' years ago*, or: *in my head I don't seem to age*. A common assumption is that the physical body envelops us – that we are inside the body, a prisoner of sorts shackled to its mortal and imperfect form – that we have a timeless essence that is at odds with the ageing body, but if so, then where exactly is this timeless core and where is its boundary? For instance, do we exist within a specific area of the body or do we exist throughout our entire body ending at the outer layer of our skin? If we lose a finger, then I am guessing the consensus is that we do not lose a small percentage of our core essence, but that we lose a small percentage of our body. So how far into the body would we need to go, how deep do we dig, before we hit that indivisible timeless centre of our being? We may localise this core essence to the head – specifically the brain – arguing that we can potentially survive a lost limb or an eye, and that organ transplants are possible, including the heart, but the brain is (*currently*) non-negotiable. So is the brain the seat of the Self, and is that where we reside?

The brain's main function is cell-to-cell communication made possible via nerve cells called synapses (around one hundred billion of them), each transmitting signals from a neuron to a target cell via chemicals called neurotransmitters. The result is an organ that is the communication centre of the body, monitoring and regulating unconscious bodily processes through the autonomic nervous system, such as breathing, heartbeat and hormones, and coordinating most voluntary movements. This organ is also understood to hold our memory and personality, and to produce thought; in this model then, the mind, consisting of memories, thoughts and feelings, is synonymous with the notion of the self, and the conscious awareness of the Self is usually internalised as a mental image of 'myself'. Research in neuroscience has mapped areas of the brain associated with reasoning, planning, movement, orientation, visual processing, memory and speech. Neurologists can even pinpoint specialist areas, such as those responsible for facial recognition. However, despite these advances in our understanding of brain function, do we feel comfortable defining ourselves purely in neurological terms? Can our deepest emotions be the result of neural connections and chemical reactions? Do we arise from the physical properties of our brains, brains that if deprived of oxygen for only a few minutes, would snuff us out like a flame deprived of air? Can we be reduced to this 3lb jelly-like mass of grey tissue? Locating the Self within or as a product of the material world describes us in terms of nerve cells, glial cells, small electrical signals and chemical messengers. However, the more neuroscience uncovers, the harder it becomes for many to relate emotionally and intuitively to the findings.

An alternative and very appealing idea for some is that of an incorporeal soul or essence inhabiting the body – something that is crucially non-physical and can therefore survive it. However, this is also problematic – for where is this soul, what are its properties and its connection to the body, and how and in what form can it exist separate from the body? Dividing the world between physical and non-physical or material and spiritual does not simplify the search for our core essence; rather, it complicates it, and the same questions remain: what is our essence, the thing that has awareness, the thing that is self-conscious, and where is it located? Some believe science has the answers, proving, or will prove, we are wholly a product of our brains (reductive materialism), while others maintain science can go only so far in defining us, and that in addition to our physical properties, there is a non-physical element to our nature. Some go further; believing we are immaterial souls born into the body temporarily inhabiting it until death, whereupon we return to a spiritual plane of existence.

I mentioned earlier that the physical body could point to the reality of our situation, because its biology does not recognise the illusionary Self, refusing to be a part of it. So what does this mean? If we take the body's basic needs – food, water and shelter – in most societies they are provided in abundance, and the infinite number of other psychological desires overlaying these basic needs usually point back to an illusionary source. Of course, striving for more than these basic physical needs by improving one's physical and emotional wellbeing, gaining knowledge and mastering new skills are natural human urges, and I'm not suggesting there is anything wrong with this – it is only when we define ourselves by those strivings and achievements that the problems begin.

Those who contemplate the apparent mind / body division often view the body as either the corporeal vessel of an immortal spirit or the physical instrument of the brain's consciousness. Either way, the body is believed to be the vehicle through which one's desires (whether spiritual or physical) can be fulfilled. Many want nothing to do with what they see as the body's decay and inevitable demise, believing they are something other than this biological organism and not at the mercy of its fragility, and therefore having or being an immaterial soul is very appealing. Alternatively, as a reaction to perceived mortality and in an attempt to find fulfilment, some people addictively consume more and more, acquiring possessions and overindulging in food and drink, often to the body's physical detriment. However, rather than being a vehicle to abuse or a constant reminder of our impermanence and fragility, the body could actually be our salvation.

Regardless of the body's physical condition, it is not striving to be anything other than it is; such impulses come from the illusionary Self as it tries to impose conceptual ideals upon the body, wanting it to be different. If the body is freed from the psychological constraints placed upon it and left to function naturally, it will find a balance embracing the darkness of pain and the brightness of pleasure, and all shades between. However, this natural functioning is not about comparing one shade to another, nor is it a spiritual acceptance of things as they are; it is beyond comparisons and acceptance – it is the raw uncompromising reality of life itself. This raw reality underpins all our egoic mind chatter and all our conceptual thoughts. The Self attempts to take ownership of the body and use it to fulfil its own needs and desires, not realising that the body is in a different paradigm, one that does not recognise the existence of the Self and so little wonder then, that there is a conflict between the actual living reality of this biological organism and the desires of the illusionary Self. The body resides in the simplicity of pure being-ness, any apparent problems are in fact the illusionary Self's problems born from its blinkered and distorted perception of the body and the world it inhabits.

Focusing on the body in this way does not reduce us to the purely physical; it raises us to the purely physical – removing the straightjacket of the distorted psyche is liberating. The individual with all its demands, desires, hopes and dreams is seen for what it is: a phantom, and we vanish. Liberation is neither comforting to the soul nor beneficial to the Self because it happens to no one. Awakening to our true nature is Liberation, which does not add to us; it peels us like an onion until there is nothing left, but that no-thing is a perfectly functioning organism requiring very little from life simply because it is life. Once liberated from the illusion, what remains needs neither imposed morality nor directions on how to live. With no effort the light of consciousness will shine through in a pure and untainted outpouring of the Absolute.

Once the Self is exposed as an illusion, existing in the emptiness left behind is a living, breathing organism pulsating with life having a physiology as astounding in its complexity as in its beauty. Freed from the individual psyche of the Self and without the egoic mind, this sentient creature has crystal-clear awareness and a pure unfiltered being-ness – a beating heart that simply is. The beauty of its form is staggering: existing as oxygen, carbon, hydrogen, nitrogen, calcium and phosphorus, forming 206 bones, 600 muscles and 22 internal organs all functioning cooperatively through multiple systems: circulatory, immune, skeletal, excretory, muscular, endocrine, digestive, nervous and respiratory. This astounding biological organism with its inconceivably complex and breath-taking structure has a pure undiluted sense of its immediate surroundings, a sentience allowing it to behold the miracle of its own existence – the universe experiencing itself. Left alone, the innate intelligence of the life force flowing through every cell of our bodies has a natural peace and serenity that is one with the deeper stillness – *the I before I am*. This life force does not end at the outer layer of our skin – it has no boundaries, no beginning or end; it is the formless eternal Absolute that animates everything.

14

CONSCIOUSNESS

Consciousness cannot be accounted for in physical terms. For consciousness is absolutely fundamental. It cannot be accounted for in terms of anything else.

ERWIN SCHRÖDINGER

Among the great things which are found among us, the Being of Nothingness is the greatest.

LEONARDO DA VINCI

That we are all conscious is something we must surely agree upon, however, despite being one of the very few things we have a shared consensus over, it is strangely very difficult to define, or at least to define in a way that finds common agreement. Its ambiguity stems from the fact that any enquiry regarding its nature seems to depend upon the context of the investigation. Philosophy, cognitive science, neuroscience and psychology each have their own approaches, and even within their own specific disciplines, there are wildly differing views and much disagreement. Proposing a definitive cross-disciplinary definition of consciousness is nigh on impossible, as the more it is investigated, the less hope there seems of finding a self-evident and generic understanding.

Most debates fall into one of two camps: physicalism or dualism, where consciousness is either physical in nature or non-physical. There are various theories within physicalism, such as identity theory and functionalism, all of which reduce consciousness to particular properties of the brain, such as specific arrangements of atoms and bundles of neurons. These theories view the brain as a complex biological computer, and the mental states emerging from it as purely physical. Dualism holds the theory that consciousness is entirely non-physical, and is either completely separate from the physical (Cartesian dualism) or arises out of physical properties (property dualism). There is a third alternative, panpsychism: the view that all things have a mind or a mind-like quality, or if you prefer, all matter is conscious. Idealism is the philosophical parallel of panpsychism, whereby ideas are the only true reality. Idealism holds that only the mental realm exists and the physical world is an illusion.

Consciousness is such a thorny subject, because although we instinctively sense what it is, it is nevertheless extremely difficult to describe and to encapsulate. Many of the difficulties in understanding come down to the fact that there is nothing to compare or contrast it with – you can only experience consciousness you cannot experience unconsciousness. In fact, experience and consciousness are one and the same. The so-called *hard problem* of consciousness (explaining the relationship between physical phenomena and experience) is born from the fact that consciousness is inextricably linked to every thought, every sensation and every experience, including all our philosophical, psychological and physiological enquiries into them, and thus we find ourselves facing the conundrum of trying to be aware of awareness. The following passage from the Kena Upanishad succinctly describes the inherent difficulty of mind grasping mind: *Just as fire that burns and enlightens things does not either enlighten or burn itself, so the mind, which wills and determines in respect of external objects, cannot will or determine in respect of its self.*

It would appear then, when trying to explain consciousness we have to define the context within which we are framing the discussion. The philosophical approach to understanding consciousness is usually to adopt an intransitive definition, and to think in terms of being self-consciously aware of awareness. Therefore, the philosopher is concerned about awareness *in and of itself* without necessarily needing an object upon which to focus that awareness. Science investigates consciousness in terms of the physical properties of the brain and how it interprets the outside world, whereas psychologists place great emphasis upon the subconscious, and the interplay between it and our conscious thoughts and actions. Perhaps most of us, if we give it any thought, are likely to describe consciousness in terms of being aware of our environment and some may go a step further and describe it as being self-aware. Self-awareness or conscious awareness appears to arise in our mind. We could describe our mind as an inner dialogue of subjective thoughts – to put it simply this inner dialogue is the voice in your head.

We talked earlier about not becoming your thoughts and about your story and its narrator: the narrator is the voice in your head that thinks and problem solves and seemingly makes decisions (free will is discussed in Chapter 17). When it comes to making choices and decisions this voice often starts counterarguments so you find you are in a bizarre internal dialogue apparently talking to yourself. In addition to arguing with itself, this voice places qualitative judgements on your perceptions and creates emotional reactions to future events, so for example, becoming anxious over an upcoming meeting with someone you dislike, or like a lot! It is difficult to explain this inner voice in terms of physical properties but despite its intangible nature, it actually feels like the solid, dependable and reliable core of your being having a familiarity and constancy that is rare in life.

This constant internal dialogue is such an integral part of how you function that you probably do not give it a second thought; but can you imagine anything more intimate, anything closer to the essence of who you are, than the voice inside your head as you read these words. If you were in any doubt then ask yourself where would you be without it. *I transcend this* tries to break the continual cycle of thought-based moments – it is a prompt for you to question the authority of that ever-present voice in your head, and hopefully in doing so drop into the deeper consciousness underpinning it. The voice in the head is your personal consciousness – your self-awareness, it is what I have been referring to as the illusionary Self. The stillness beneath is the deeper consciousness – the voiceless *I before I am*. *I transcend this is* a sort of Trojan horse that offers itself to the illusionary Self as a gift and then attacks it from within; if the phrase is meditated upon in the moment, then the thoughts that sustain the illusionary Self are seen through and the deeper consciousness gets temporary relief from the stranglehold thought.

For now, let us investigate this inner voice from the perspective of our day-to-day experience. What then is the source of the inner voice reading these words right now? Where does it originate, and what is its relationship to you – or is it you? Are you reading these words to yourself and if so does that mean there are two entities: one reading and another listening? When thinking, does the thought arise first then spoken by this inner voice, or are they one and the same? Does the voice in your head 'sound' like your speaking voice; does it have the same accent and modulation, pitch and tone – does it stay the same over the years? We discussed the mind/body split in the previous chapter and similarly, we could ask the same dualistic question: is this inner voice a non-physical soul/spirit hosted by a material body, or an evolutionary advantageous result of natural selection – a consciousness arising from the brain – a specific neural network firing in the neocortex? When investigating this matter, it is difficult to make progress, because although the inner voice seems to be at your core, it has no physical properties: it has no shape, colour, taste or smell, and most peculiarly for a voice, no sound in the sense that (thankfully) it cannot be heard by anyone else. Despite having no discernible physical properties it reflects your conscious awareness back to you, perhaps the closest to who and what you believe you are. We will pick this up a little later, but for now let us simplify the challenge of attempting to be aware of awareness and instead settle upon a transitive definition of consciousness, as being aware of and responsive to one's surroundings. With this definition in mind, let us explore consciousness from a physiological perspective, specifically a medical one concerning responsiveness, alertness and comprehension.

If a doctor is presented with a patient whose vital signs are stable but suffers from physical trauma following an accident leaving them unresponsive to external stimulus (the patient does not answer to their name or show any signs of communication/is unresponsive to pain), they are likely to be diagnosed as unconscious. Let us suppose this patient subsequently regains consciousness several hours later, and tries recalling what happened. They remember events leading up to the trauma, but there is a gap in their memory from a short time before the accident, until they regain consciousness in hospital. This gap, this missing time, may never be recovered. The same sense of missing time occurs under general anaesthetic. Anyone who has been given a general anaesthetic will know that no sooner is the anaesthetic administered, then it will seem that they are waking up in recovery, disorientated, groggy, and often bemused as to what just happened. When unconscious or under general anaesthetic, there is no awareness of the external environment nor any self-awareness, since there is no discernible individual Self present. There is also no awareness of time passing, and afterwards there are no memories to recall because there was no experience recorded. Thus the unconscious time simply does not exist.

This is nothing unusual, as every night each of us enters this state of non-awareness, when time stands still and memory cannot recall in deep sleep (or delta sleep): a dreamless sleep state outside of REM sleep where electroencephalograms (EEGs) record increased delta brainwaves. You are not unconscious in the medical sense but nonetheless, there is a loss of awareness as the body falls into a controlled sleep state. When in a state of unconsciousness following physical trauma, under general anaesthetic or in deep sleep, there is no awareness of a personal I or a Self and the inner voice is silenced, so where exactly are you at these times? Obviously your body goes nowhere, and so in the physical sense you are wherever your body rests. However, there is no self-awareness – no voice in the head. Where does that leave the core of your being, your essence – your Self? Perhaps you are suspended in an empty void waiting to wake up, but waiting requires both duration in time and a subjective awareness of its passage, neither of which is experienced – nothing is experienced, or more precisely, there is no experience. If you can simply disappear in the blink of an eye, and then through no will of your own reappear some time later, how in control are you? How solid and dependable is this awareness – this personal consciousness, how real and how permanent are you?

From the moment we are born, light floods in through our eyes firing signals from the retina to the brain, illuminating our inner world. We build an internal model from the information streaming in through our senses, allowing us to interact with the external world, and gradually through our conditioning the concept of a Self (an I) overlays this raw awareness, creating the duality of perceiver and perceived. We assume it is the Self that perceives – that we are subjectively seeing – when in fact there is just seeing with no one (no-thing) viewing. However, common sense insists that for there to be sight, there must be something that sees, and if it is not the Self, then what is it? One could say it is consciousness that sees, but that simply shifts attention to another thing, a thing that is incredibly difficult to investigate, because *it* is doing the investigation. Here I will use darkness as a metaphor in an attempt to overcome this impasse. Despite darkness being a very emotive word with mainly negative connotations, it may help to show why consciousness is so hard to pin down and why searching for it is self-defeating.

Darkness is not a thing in and of itself; rather, it is an absence of something else, namely light. Darkness cannot be seen. A windowless room is in darkness until the light is switched on, whereupon we see its contents: a table and four chairs, a picture on the wall, etc., but we do not see the darkness. Darkness is not a thing. Light does not reveal the darkness; instead, it removes it by illuminating things, such as tables and chairs. Using the intellect in an attempt to recognise consciousness is like shining a torch in an attempt to see darkness: we will reveal all manner of things but not the darkness they are held within. To put it another way: using the intellect to search for truth you will only find phenomena – the underlying truth disappears when the light of our enquiry falls upon it. Conversely, if when enquiring into the Self we do so by entering the darkness without our intellectual torchlight, we are actually returning home – embracing unknowing and the emptiness of non-being. The impossibility of knowing that which 'sees', should not blind one to the joys of living with all its pure sensual delights, indeed if one can live life with an awareness that there is no 'personal experiencing' but simply 'experiencing', and sense that all manifestations are born from the same impersonal emptiness, then such delights are multiplied ten-fold. When life is not polluted by selfishness or Self interest it becomes pure joy.

The trap many spiritual seekers fall into is, having embraced a personal consciousness (an illusionary Self) they assume that increasing self-awareness or expanding one's consciousness will bring them closer to the truth of their being. The idea that the Self is able to move towards a greater awareness or higher consciousness is flawed; this restricted personal consciousness (the illusionary Self) does not hold the key to its own liberation, quite the opposite. Because consciousness is usually associated with personal identity and therefore personal feelings and desires, attempting to expand it into something greater will only strengthen the illusion of the individual. Using personal consciousness in the pursuit of the Absolute will bring you no nearer to the truth of your being; like the dog chasing its own tail, you will be sent in circles. Personal consciousness (the illusionary Self) is a distortion of the Absolute – it is a flawed perspective of the source that animates all. The Absolute is a stream of pure consciousness – it is *the I before I am*; as discussed previously, the illusionary Self is the result of mistaken identity.

So retuning to the voice in the head let us imagine for a moment that we can see from the perspective of the Absolute. From this vantage point, the voice is your conditioned thoughts, the language and logic it employs has been taught, and its phrasing and vocabulary is a reflection of your education and experiences (discussed further in the next chapter). These conditioned thoughts perpetuate the illusionary Self; they are not an expression of your immediate environment or your physiology. In other words, pure conscious awareness is distorted by the story of you and its narrator, which filters your perceptions and imposes your own reality upon the world thereby missing the clarity of the present moment. This deeper non-verbal hidden realm is not touched by the surface level experiences of daily life; it is your story that personalises those experiences thus creating duality and suffering. For some, this deeper awareness is a faint echo, and for others it is a way of being, but whether it is strong or weak, it lies at the heart of everyone – the underlying animating force that gives rise to all.

As mentioned earlier, this animating force has many names, Lao Tzu called it 'the Tao', Buddha called it 'Emptiness', Jesus called it 'The Kingdom of Heaven' and said it is within you, and many contemporary spiritual masters call it 'Pure Conscious Awareness' or 'Divine Presence' or simply 'Consciousness'. Of course, these are all just words and as such can only point to the truth – *the Tao that can be spoken is not the true Tao*. The animating force flowing through us is impossible to define, but if it must be named then something as mysterious as consciousness is as good a word as any, however this pure conscious awareness is impossible to know because it lies outside conceptual understanding, not only pointing beyond the material world but also giving rise to the material world. It is the eternal subject and we are the objects perceived in its light. I will conclude this chapter with a beautiful Rumi poem, which I believe encapsulates the idea of consciousness working through us:

Who are we, O Thou soul of our souls,
that we should remain in being beside thee?
We and our existences are really non-existence;
thou art the absolute Being which manifests the perishable.
We all are lions, but lions on a banner:
because of the wind they are rushing onward from moment to moment.
Their onward rush is visible, and the wind is unseen:
may that which is unseen not fail from us!
Our wind whereby we are moved and our being are of thy gift;
our whole existence is from thy bringing into being.

RUMI

15

INDOCTRINATION

Some people will never learn anything, for this reason, because they understand everything too soon.

ALEXANDER POPE

When thy heart shall have worked through the snares of delusion, then thou wilt attain to high indifference as to those doctrines which are already taught or which are yet to be taught.

BHAGAVAD-GITA

Education is an admirable thing, but it is well to remember from time to time that nothing that is worth knowing can be taught.

OSCAR WILDE

INDOCTRINATION

Most of us will have been through a compulsory education system, some readers will still be in that system, such conditioning allows us to function both socially and professionally through shared values, mutual aspirations and common goals and objectives. Indeed, so ingrained is the educational ethic that students are willingly to pay for higher education in order to improve their status and give a competitive edge over their peers, gone are the days when higher education was about the love of learning and gaining wisdom – its now more like a business transaction that leaves the student in debt. Creating individuals who fit society's norms requires uniform conditioning, the idea being the stronger the conditioning, the more productive and the less problematic those individuals will be. Of course, it is not called conditioning it is called 'education'. Because of the structure of society, there is no doubt that without at least a basic education you are at a great disadvantage in terms of gaining employment.

For all these reasons, our young are enrolled into the education system as early as possible (pre-school is available and encouraged from the age of two in most countries) and with a strong logical and methodical left-brain bias the production line starts. Home schooling is discouraged in favour of state-run schools, following a strict set of rules known as the National Curriculum. Private schools, also known as independent schools or non-state schools, are an option for some; they do not have to follow the National

Curriculum but must be registered with the government and are regularly inspected, and their pupils are tested against the same benchmarks as state schools. Any parents or guardians wishing to home school their children may have to justify their choice, and accept some form of monitoring. The level of regulatory difficulty parents' encounter in home schooling will depend upon the country or the state in which they live, it is not made easy because society requires like-minded individuals not freethinkers or nonconformists, and that requires centrally controlled collective indoctrination.

Within the school system, any open and questioning minds are systematically broken down, reprogrammed and then tested against benchmark standards. Those who measure up are rewarded with high grades and progression, while those who fight the system or are unable to regurgitate in the prescribed ways are failed and held back. The fear of exclusion created by an inability to understand what others 'appear' to understand is a pernicious and negative driving force in the collective indoctrination of students. The emotional scars such a forced education leaves can be deep, and many adults live in the shadow of stressful and negative educational experiences. The child's schooling is relentless and lasts into adulthood, giving plenty of time to brainwash thoroughly. Ironically, during the whole process of force-feeding a standard education and shared values, the students are ostensibly encouraged to think for themselves, and to demonstrate their individuality and creativity. However, those who follow this advice a little too enthusiastically, soon realise they have to work within an acceptable framework, since any ideas or indeed actions that threaten the status quo are quickly smothered. This eventually confirms to those of a rebellious nature what was in hindsight obvious: the most important attribute needed to survive school is conformity.

Ironically, those who are the most successful in their creative endeavours following school are often the outsiders and nonconformists, producing work or following creative paths that give people a taste of something different. However, for every successful artist, numerous others are broken on the wheel of conformity. Throughout their schooling, students are closely monitored as they walk this prescribed line between compliance and creativity. Those who are able to closely repeat what has been taught, and can demonstrate their individuality (within the acceptable limits) proudly accept their certificates of achievement, and are supposedly better able to integrate into society and achieve success. This is the only path available to most people, which is hardly surprising, since those in positions of power and influence have previously succeeded in the very same system, and therefore securing its continuity is in their best interest. Indeed, teachers and administrators are also closely monitored and evaluated, ensuring they too conform to the same system.

Having, hopefully, passed all the tests, you leave school with not only society's approval but also an understanding of society's expectations: you fit in and are in a good position to find fulfilment and happiness – or so you are led to believe. The cracks only start appearing when it is gradually realised that everything you have accomplished – everything – has come from outside, nothing has come from within and that your self-image is built upon, other people's values, personal achievements, possessions and peer recognition. This sometimes becomes apparent early on in life but is more likely to happen following a loss, perhaps financial, or ill health, or loss of a loved one. Sometimes all it takes is reaching middle age and the realisation that the years ahead of you are fewer than those you have lived. It can be a difficult and confusing time because at no point during your education has the subject of self-enquiry been raised, in fact, such investigation is not even recognised. Instead, you have been pointed in the opposite direction – you are taught to accumulate external knowledge and regurgitate facts and figures, relying upon the logical left-brain world of the sciences. It is only when the fruits of your education taste sour, and the promised fulfilment and happiness does not materialise that you begin to question your life.

Looking within and questioning your motives, your goals and the conditioning that created them, may reveal why any resulting achievements never transfer to your inner world in a fulfilling or meaningful way and why, contrary to what you have been taught, deep down inside there is nothing that seems the least bit interested in them. We are all familiar with longing for something and wanting it so intensely you can't stop thinking about it, imagining over and over what it would be like to have, and then when it becomes a reality and it is finally ours, what happens? The initial elation is slowly replaced with that familiar depressive slump, as you realise it has not changed a damn thing; it has not touched you, let alone brought lasting happiness. You have been led to believe these external trappings are necessary and that in order to possess them you must work towards certain goals. However, once those goals are attained there is no lasting fulfilment, quite the opposite – there is just a deep unease because nothing inside seems to have benefited. You therefore assume that something more is needed and so the pattern is repeated as the next goal is set and chased after.

After years or even decades, you may eventually tire of the chase, and come to a kind of standstill. However, that brings its own problems, because you are then left with a nagging feeling that you have not reached your full potential, and life is passing you by. The perception of living a mundane life can fuel this feeling of underachievement, and years of conformity and suppression can lead to neurotic behaviour, depression and sometimes self-destructive thoughts and actions. Life's casualties are all around us – the homeless person huddled on the street corner or a close friend or family member suffering from depression, but there are many more hiding in plain sight. Scratch the surface of society's supposedly well-adjusted and successful people, and you will uncover individuals battling with extreme personal torments and debilitating inner conflicts as they fight to hold on to their self-image – desperately trying to 'keep it together' by attempting to fill the emptiness at their core.

Education has a strong emphasis upon external aims and objectives, and reaching those objectives becomes a measure of your success. However, through reflection and contemplation, the need to achieve those goals may feel false and achievements may ring hollow, and so your focus may dwell more and more within as you question exactly what you want from life, aside from what you have been socially conditioned to want. When it comes to questioning one's Self, there is no guidance within the standard educational system, and those who attempt such enquiry naturally fall back on the left brain analytical problem-solving skills they have been taught – skills they will find are completely ineffective. In addition to using the wrong tools, you are also actively discouraged from asking such questions and, as mentioned, the focus is always directed towards interacting most effectively with the outside world; the false assumption being that if you get that right, then inner peace and fulfilment follows.

Philosophy (from the Ancient Greek *philosophia: love of wisdom*) is as close as it gets to an academic discipline that enquires into the nature of reality and existence. However, it is not compulsory in schools, and usually focuses upon a narrow band of Western thinkers with an emphasis less upon self-enquiry, and more upon the ability to memorise and regurgitate standard texts. Interest in philosophy is further hampered by the fact that it is often portrayed as a marginalised pursuit for the introspective loner. This is unfortunate, because by the time most individuals begin to ponder difficult issues such as mortality, free will, meaning and the nature of the Self, it is virtually impossible to find satisfactory answers using left-brain logic and methodology. Unlike other subjects where you are dissecting and re-evaluating the known, to make progress here you have to embrace the unknown.

To investigate and question the Self – *which I suggest is central to all philosophical enquiry* – you must first focus your attention upon what exactly is attempting the investigation. You must not assume to have a solid starting position – you have to take a step back rather than a step forward. You have to begin disassembling not only what you have been taught, but also the methodical problem-solving skills you have learned. This is nicely portrayed in the story of the Japanese Zen master Nan-in who, during the Meiji era (1868–1912), received a university professor enquiring about Zen. Before beginning their discourse, the professor is first encouraged to drop his accumulated knowledge:

> *Nan-in served tea. He poured his visitor's cup full, and then kept on pouring. The professor watched the overflow until he no longer could restrain himself.*
>
> *'It is overfull. No more will go in!'*
>
> *'Like this cup,' Nan-in said, 'you are full of your own opinions and speculations. How can I show you Zen unless you first empty your cup?'*

Self-enquiry is about less, not more. It is about taking away, not adding to – about the absence of things, not the addition of more things. As pointed out previously, to confuse the logical mind still further, introspection is paradoxical since we are asking something illusionary to investigate itself in an attempt to expose its illusionary nature (discussed further in the following chapter). One could ask if we are successful and the illusionary Self is exposed, then what exactly has it been exposed to – what sees through the illusion? These questions highlight the difficulties investigating the Self using our ingrained analytical skills and problem-solving methodologies. To break free from those thought patterns and get a flavour of the indescribable being-ness behind everything, our language has to adopt a more poetic approach. Analogies, metaphors and poems hope to resonate with an innate knowing. Of course, the mind trained in left-brain reasoning will expect logically coherent argument and empirically verifiable facts, and will give little importance to resonance or innate knowing. Poetic language will be viewed as neither true nor false but rather as meaningless. If, however, the mind is freed from its accumulated knowledge and the straight jacket of thought, then feeling a resonance or a shared vibrational energy can produce profound insights. Self-enquiry has to begin by realising you have been taught how to think, and then told what to think. Realise you are investigating from a closed mind running a programmed script – realise you have been indoctrinated. Therefore, you must first 'empty your cup' before true enquiry can begin.

16

SELF ENQUIRY

Meditation is the dissolution of thoughts in Eternal awareness or Pure consciousness without objectification, knowing without thinking, merging finitude in infinity.

VOLTAIRE

To study the self is to forget the self. To forget the self is to be actualised by myriad things ... your body and mind as well as the bodies and minds of others drop away. No trace of realisation remains, and this no-trace continues endlessly.

DOGEN ZENJI

SELF ENQUIRY

The illusionary Self lives in the past with an eye on the future because it is never satisfied with the present. It feels safe in the known and fears the unknown; therefore, it does everything it can to plan and secure a future out of the unknown. It hopes past experiences can inform choices that will lead to future fulfilment and happiness. For most seekers, self-enquiry is approached with the same rationale: as a means to an end, a future awakening, a future of happiness and peace built on the experience of the past. However, the bedrock of its investigation – *its own reality* – is never questioned. Built on shaky foundations it investigates concepts that promise to bring meaning and purpose, but with no solid base any spiritual understandings crumble under the slightest pressure. Because the investigation is from a false perspective, it is that viewpoint – *the illusionary Self* – we have been investigating. '*What lies behind us and what lies before us are tiny matters compared to what lies within us*' (Ralph Waldo Emerson). Recognising that an intellectual search conducted by an illusionary Self will simply add another dead concept to our stories can led to a fundamental shift in attention whereby the investigative spotlight turns 180 degrees.

Turning the bright spotlight to face you is initially painful – the natural reaction is to avert the eyes, however, illuminating our thoughts and the story it maintains reveals the illusion of the Self, allowing a new clarity to emerge from a deeper level of being. The phrase *I transcend this* (introduced in Chapter 7) is an attempt to turn the mind back upon itself and question the truth of our thought-based reality. By continually focusing on your personal story and how it drives your thinking and directs your life, and how virtually all your suffering is generated by past stories and future projections (most of which are negative), you begin to see that your bedrock is a complex web of thoughts sparking conflicting, contradictory and confusing emotions. What hope for peace? All your efforts are focused upon trying to navigate this complex web of internal feelings and emotions in an attempt to make the 'right' choices and say and do the 'right' things, and while all your energy is consumed in the labyrinths of your mind you miss the beauty happening around you. Leaving behind such madness using *I transcend this* allows you to witness your insane mind games and brings moments of stillness beyond concepts. Regardless of how hard the egoic mind fights to maintain its reality, the floodgates to the deeper truth will start to open, spelling the beginning of the end for the illusionary Self.

All that actually exists is the pure presence of the Absolute – *the I before I am*. This unknowable emptiness gives rise to all, including the illusion of searching, the difficulty understanding, the desire to understand and any ambivalence, frustration or realisation. It is the formless underlying all forms, the source of all; you cannot know it because you are it, it is so proximate you cannot see it. At one level of understanding, the Absolute can be likened to a pair of reading glasses: The glasses function by being so close that you do not see them – you see through them. If you need to work on the glasses, for instance if the hinges need adjusting, you have to remove them. You are then separated from their function and they have become an object of enquiry. However, now your vision is blurred making it impossible to do the work, thus you find yourself in the frustrating situation whereby what you want to see is what makes the seeing possible. Similarly, attempting to turn the Absolute into an object of enquiry you attempt to distance yourself from it, which creates an illusionary separation and the truth is blurred. You cannot see the absolute because it is doing the seeing.

To add to the difficulties, articulating the direct experience of the Absolute is impossible. Language relies upon naming and discriminating between things to give common symbols (written and verbal) with which to communicate, all of which are ineffective when experiencing the indivisible. Those who want to know it – to confirm its existence and describe it – are perpetuating separation and thus remain firmly within the illusion of a separate Self. The Self cannot know the Absolute and neither can the Absolute know itself, because to do so the indivisible would have to split into that which knows (the subject) and that which is known (the object). We have come to see that true self-enquiry is not a process of adding to your understanding nor is it about personal growth, it is about dropping your story and letting go of your preconceptions, it is about witnessing your mind games with a sort of compassionate detachment. *Approach it and there is no beginning; follow it and there is no end. You cannot know it, but you can be it, at ease in your own life. Just realize where you come from: this is the essence of wisdom* (Tao Te Ching).

Take a step back from your thinking mind. Keep stepping back, and when you think you are at the source step back once more. When the search is dropped and stillness is embraced the Absolute is glimpsed; caught in a movement, or heard in a sound – held for a breath, a beat of the heart. True in the moment until falsified by thought, alive in unknowing until deadened by language. It comes before all, underpinning everything, here in plain view, reflecting back every named phenomenon and every experience. Infinite are the ways the Self searches for truth: philosophy, theology, psychology and sociology. Such pursuits may increase knowledge and intellectual understanding but are of no use when seeking the Absolute – its truth cannot be conceptualised. As previously discussed, you have been taught how to think, and this process is so ingrained that usually only concepts matching existing thought patterns will be recognised and embraced (Analogies can help in this regard and there are a selection in the appendix). The intellect cannot discern truth; it cannot be taught or understood; a lifetime accumulating knowledge and refining ideas and beliefs will move you not a step closer.

The individual who yearns for truth and Liberation, is caught in a trap analogous to the following story: It is said that there's an ingenious method of catching monkeys using a large clay pot tied to a tree. The story goes that a poacher places an apple inside the pot that has an opening slightly larger than a monkey's hand and then hides in waiting. Patience is often rewarded as a monkey approaches and smelling the fruit squeezes its hand into the pot grabbing the apple and making a fist that is too large to retract. Despite having the means to escape by simply letting go it tightens its grip, even as the poacher breaks cover, the wretched animal remains trapped by its desire for the fruit and is subsequently caught. You may feel a mixture of pity and irritation towards the unfortunate creature: if only it could see things differently, if only it could see the bigger picture all its suffering would be over in an instant.

We are clutching at life, our desires imprison us; freedom is letting go. We search relentlessly for a truth that will set us free and only by letting go do we recognise the tragicomedy of our lives: We were led to believe that truth and freedom from suffering was a reward after a lifetime of one hundred thousand steps, when in actual fact they were available in each step we took – available to us from the very beginning by simply letting go.

Self-enquiry will inevitably bring you back to where you started: right here at the source and ground of your being – the place you never left. *We shall not cease from exploration and the end of all our exploring will be to arrive where we started and know the place for the first time* (T. S. Eliot). It is simple not complicated. It is effortless not difficult. It is dropping not carrying – letting go not clutching. This ever-present source precedes everything and desires nothing. It is the stillness found once the mind is quietened and the present moment is allowed to simply be.

17

FATE AND FREE WILL

Do you think I know what I am doing? That for one breath I belong to myself? As much as a pen knows what it is writing or the ball can guess where it is going next.

RUMI

One of the questions I keep getting is 'So what you are saying is that I can't do anything, and that I have no responsibility?' And I keep on repeating: 'No, I am not saying you can't do anything, because that would imply that there is someone who can't do anything.'

TONY PARSONS

If we are all manifestations of the one inseparable and immovable timeless source what implications does that have upon our actions and the consequences of those actions – where does that leave one of the things we seem to cherish the most: our free will? Acknowledging that every thought and action is a manifestation of the Absolute, then to do nothing, could simply imply not getting out of bed in the morning, not caring for ourselves and loved ones. So what is our mandate for acting in the world, as opposed to not bothering and laying down to die? I would suggest that a recognition of our relationship to the Absolute will make any actions natural and Self-less. However, this should not be confused with trying to act selflessly, which will only reinforce the illusionary Self. This is more akin to the Bhagavad Gita's advice not to stop acting in the world, but to make our actions holy. I believe that 'holy' in this context means recognition of something greater than our Self; a deep reservoir of pure consciousness from which we are the surface springs.

For the vast majority the sense of being an individual Self is lived as a reality and that reality includes trying to manage and take control of life by making the right decisions and taking the right actions. You may rationalise that once in control, you are more likely to acquire and retain the things you want, and the experiences you desire, and avoid those you dislike. The assumption is that once the right balance is achieved and everything is exactly as it should be, and there are no more worries or concerns, then happiness will follow. However, this never happens, certainly not for any length of time. You believe you must gain control to affect outcomes and bring about desired change, but the more you try to take control and manipulate life, the more you suffer. Eventually it may become apparent that you are not, and never were, in control of life, and that actually it seems as if life is in control of you. However, this realisation is never fully accepted, and the struggle to tame life continues along with the inevitable suffering in trying to do so.

After many years fighting a losing battle, your beleaguered Self may eventually ask for help, and since it is not uncommon to do so there is a plethora of support available in various guises: counsellors, psychologists, psychiatrists, clergy, teachers, gurus, these resources can be accessed in person, in print or online. Not forgetting the group whose unquestionable sincerity is matched only by their unhelpfulness: well-meaning friends. Unless the support is coming from a nondual/transpersonal perspective it will, at best, bring only temporary relief, and in the long run will spin into more complex problems as life unfolds with complete indifference to your hopes and expectations. And, of course, those offering support – friends and professionals alike – are not immune to the pressures of living, they suffer just as much (sometimes more) than those they are trying to help. Indeed, many find an escape from their own maladies by helping others. The idea that mental health professionals, men and women of God and Gurus live balanced and well-adjusted lives, and that within a bubble of objectivity, they can help others live theirs, is wishful thinking. However, those desperate to find a way out of the apparent chaos need to believe there are such people and that they have the answers.

While acknowledging there is little you can do about certain unforeseen events, you may assume you are ultimately in control of your life, believing fate is in your own hands. So, for instance, if you are innocently involved in a road traffic accident, you will rationalise you were in the wrong place at the wrong time. If you are diagnosed with a serious illness, you may question your genetics and your lifestyle. If you sprain your ankle in a fall, you may query your balance, agility and alertness, but apart from bad timing, bad genes and bad luck, you will most likely believe it is you in charge, and therefore finding happiness and success is ultimately in your hands.

Your views regarding fate or destiny will depend upon your attitude towards decision-making, specifically your belief in free will. Having freedom of choice and the ability to make independent decisions is rarely questioned, but if given some thought, you may find there is something similar about all the decisions you appear to be making. Each one depends upon numerous other factors outside of your control, and often seems to be made despite you rather than because of you. If you try to find the origin of any single decision, it is not straightforward, because there is always a preceding decision, action or influence that led to it, and that preceding decision will be dependent upon a previous one, which in turn will be dependent upon another and so on. Backtracking to find the source it is not as simple as retracing your footprints in the sand, it is incredibly complex and totally futile because of the endless trail of decisions and influences. Unpicking them to find the source would be like trying to retrace your footprints having kicked a ball around for an hour on the beach.

You may disagree with what is being proposed here, believing you have freedom to make independent decisions. So let us imagine that to prove your point, you decide to close this book and read no further. *Assuming you are still here*, would that action have been a free and independent decision? Firstly, in order to stop reading the book, you obviously had to be in possession of it. So how did that come about? Why did you choose this particular book? What triggered that decision? Perhaps a friend recommended it, or gave it as a gift; if so, did you control how they entered your life or their actions? If you stumbled upon it in a bookstore or through a random online search, why did this particular book catch your attention? Why did this specific subject area interest you, and what sparked that interest? What were the early influences that led to your curiosity, and how much control did you have over those influences? Throughout your life, have you had any control over the people who enter it, and how they affect you? Did you have control over how you were schooled or by whom, or over how you were nurtured as an infant? Is it plausible that you made a conscious decision to read this book free from any preceding influences or personal preferences? This example only scratches the surface of the countless influences, conditioned responses and subsequent actions that have led you here. There are an infinite number of such factors, and an infinite number of influences preceding every single decision you apparently make.

One could argue that all these preceding influences only provide a backdrop to the current moment, and that you still have the freedom of choice to make independent decisions – decisions isolated from all preceding factors, but is the background leading up to this moment separate from the decision, or is it integral to it? Can your actions really be independent from what went before? We find ourselves in this specific situation living this particular life; however, looking back, we may wonder exactly how we have arrived here, and question whether we chose this specific path for ourselves? We certainly did not choose our parents, and during infancy all the choices were made for us. As we grow, we appear to start making decisions but the foundations of those decisions have already been laid down by the experiences of our formative years, and as young people our significant others can subtly affect the decisions we make. By the time we are adults, we take pride in being independent freethinkers, but perhaps all our apparent choices are simply the reactive responses of a fixed personality forged by circumstance. Could all the decisions we make be the inevitable consequence of the sum total of our histories to date?

Supposing for a moment, we accept the view that we are all part of an interconnecting web in which we only appear to be making decisions, and that there is actually no freedom of choice. Since any actions resulting from our predetermined decisions/choices must also be predetermined, how can we be held accountable for their consequences? What are the implications of a predestined life upon personal responsibility and accountability? So for example, if a drunk driver mounts the pavement and kills a pedestrian, surely it is the driver's actions – *namely getting behind the wheel when drunk* – that caused the fatality. The driver should expect to be judged by the laws of the society in which he lives and be punished accordingly. He could plead not guilty, arguing that he had no choice other than to drink and drive on that fateful night, and that in fact both his fate and the victim's fate were part of an 'interconnected universal unfolding' in which individual choice is an illusion. Such a plea is more likely to question the defendant's sanity than lead to his acquittal. Not only is it common sense but also part of the fabric of a civilised society that individuals are responsible for their actions, and those judged to have caused another's suffering or death (or to have otherwise broken the law) must be brought to justice. Depending upon the time, the place and the nature of the crime, the punishment may be a fine, a custodial sentence, or the offender may even pay with their life. These are society's rules of law and those who break them can expect to pay society's price. The accused may continue to protest his innocence arguing that his actions were predestined, but of course the same reasoning can be applied to the actions of the jury who subsequently arrive at a guilty verdict, and the judge who hands down the sentence.

The issue of personal responsibility for one's actions is interesting. The legal system has the ability to recognise a defendant's actions as *non compos mentis* (not of sound mind) and lessen the punishment or acquit accordingly, but to do so, the defence has to prove that at the time of the crime, the defendant's judgement was so impaired that they could not distinguish right from wrong. As you might expect, there are a multitude of further considerations when building such a defence, but the fact is that the law in most societies allows the potential acquittal of a defendant by essentially recognising that under certain conditions (technically: duress of circumstance), they cannot be held fully accountable for their actions. Despite the very stringent criteria that have to be met for such a plea, there are cases that are successfully defended in this way – usually involving a plea of diminished responsibility. So in the previous example of the drunk driver, the law will consider the circumstances leading to the fatality. Suppose the driver had a clean licence with no history of drink driving or alcohol abuse, and let us suppose on that particular night he received a call telling him his wife had been rushed to hospital following a suspected heart attack. Let us also suppose that prior to receiving the shocking news, the defendant was on his second whiskey after a bad day at the office. Having received the fateful call, his only thought was getting to the hospital as fast as possible to see his wife and so, grabbing his coat and car keys, he sets off.

Can we judge him by a single action alone, namely getting behind the wheel when drunk, or should we ask why he acted in the manner he did – especially when it was totally out of character for him to do so? Do we look at the factors preceding his decision to drive, and consider those as mitigating circumstances? If a mixture of alcohol and shock had not impaired his judgement, he may not have found himself behind the wheel of his car, and the pedestrian would have lived. That is a big if; nevertheless, perhaps these considerations should lead to a reduced sentence if such mitigating circumstances were successfully argued. If on the other hand, he was banned from driving because of a previous drink-driving offence, and was driving that night following a day of heavy drinking, should the sentence reflect those facts? Of course, in the second scenario one could investigate the reasons behind his alcoholism, and all the factors that led to it, which might complicate things still further. We may discover that his alcoholism is due to feelings of guilt and helplessness, following the loss of his son to cancer and the subsequent breakdown of his marriage years before. Let us also suppose the night in question would have been his son's 18th birthday, and he was drinking to escape the pain.

These examples of personal accountability framed within a legal context highlight the limitations in judging people's actions in isolation, and show that events and circumstances leading up to the action should be taken into consideration: did those influences affect the individual's subsequent actions in a way that diminishes or removes their responsibility? If we accept that in certain situations they do, then personal responsibility in those cases is a judgement call. If we recognise that sometimes an individual has little choice other than to act in a particular way and is therefore not responsible for their actions, and if we accept that in another scenario an individual can be held partly responsible due to certain mitigating circumstances, and in yet another is deemed fully responsible, we have introduced a sliding scale of accountability. In civilised societies, it is the law that decides where on the scale a defendant is placed, and the scale is heavily weighted in favour of personal accountability (not least because most people believe they would have exercised better judgement in a similar situation). Certain actions will be judged as good or bad, right or wrong, moral or immoral, but perhaps they are all links in an infinite chain of actions and reactions each following on from the other. This does not mean that individuals can act with impunity, because accountability for the consequences of those actions and any subsequent punishments are links in the very same chain.

Despite these arguments for a deterministic nature to decision-making, common sense screams that surely at any given moment there are an infinite number of choices we can freely make, and therefore an infinite number of potential futures we can create. Returning to the example of *deciding* to close the book; you could argue that regardless of all the historical influences, actions and reactions preceding that decision, you nevertheless made a free choice at that specific moment in time, a decision made in total isolation and unaffected by any previous psychological or subconscious influences – a pure untainted action. Can we make such impartial decisions from within a vacuum of objectivity? Is there an area of our brain – a corner of our mind – a part of our soul – that is separate and isolated from everything else and enables such decisions, or should the alternative be considered: that we are part of a unified whole within which all events are inextricably linked?

The idea that our lives are predestined (if accepted) can lead to an overall acceptance of how things are, along with the assumption that to fight against it is pointless. However, there is distinction to be made here between accepting 'what is', and giving up. Accepting 'what is' recognises that a deeper consciousness is acting through us and that free will is an illusion created after the action. The idea that we can end our struggles by simply allowing life to take us where it wishes, often described as *'going with the flow'*, is misguided; the struggles each of us face in our daily lives – all the frustrations, heartache, failures and triumphs are part of life. We cannot sanitise that life by choosing to give up and go with the flow. Such a decision is meaningless anyway because we are not in the flow – the flow is in us, – or, more precisely, we are the flow. Choosing to 'go with the flow' falsely assumes that, firstly, there is a Self that can choose, and secondly, there is a separate flow it can 'go' with.

If everything is interconnected, and all our decisions are made from a network of antecedents, where does that leave free will? From within the illusion of the separate Self it appears we make decisions and that those decisions sometimes have positive effects and sometimes have negative effects. Acting from a deeper awareness where 'doing' is replaced by 'being' and where we are fully present in the moment will bring right action because we are in tune with the deeper reality – *the I before I am*. Therefore, paradoxically, we must give time and consideration to important decisions in an effort to live as best we can, whilst realising that everything we do is the expression of the Absolute. '*Act as if there is free will, knowing that there is no such thing ... live as if you are responsible, knowing that the totality is responsible for everything. Events happen, deeds are done, but there is no individual doer thereof*' (Ramesh Balsekar).

18

TO BE AND NOT TO BE

Sometimes naked, sometimes mad, now as scholars, now as fools; thus they appear on the earth – the free ones!

RUMI

To be and not to be.
Here and now; enough,
Nothing more,
Nowhere else,
Everything here.
Inexplicable physiology,
Breathing, beating heart,
Untouched by mind, time or hope.
Here in sharp focus,
There – your life a blur.
Preceding all,
Holding all,
Empty of hope, pregnant with possibility.
Seeing, not searching,
Beholding, not looking,
Being, not doing.
Simple,
Indescribable,
Obvious,
Joy.

COLIN McMORRAN

TO BE AND NOT TO BE

As mentioned throughout this book, in an attempt to fill the void inside, most people search outside, acquiring possessions, gaining knowledge and indulging their appetites. The realisation that bodily pleasures are short-lived and ultimately unfulfilling, and that intellectual knowledge is equally unrewarding, prompts many to search in a different direction. As discussed, often our material and intellectual pursuits are replaced by spiritual ones in the belief that turning away from outside distractions and focusing upon a deeper inner search will bring greater meaning to our lives. The highest material goals are usually unrealistic and unaffordable dreams, whereas the highest spiritual ones are presented as freely available to anyone with the right attitude of mind. Of all the spiritual goals, Enlightenment is the pinnacle. It promises transcendence, transformation, truth and liberation.

Let us assume for the sake of argument, that there is such a thing as Enlightenment and that it can be attained. If there are rare individuals who at some point in their life can legitimately claim to have become Enlightened, what are the implications of such a statement? For someone to attain Enlightenment, they would initially have to be in an unenlightened state, but that begs the question: do we enter this world unenlightened, and if so is that our natural state? Whatever a newborn baby's awareness is (and I do not think we can never know), I would suggest that it is not unenlightened but that gradually and inescapably it becomes unenlightened as it grows; the same sentiment as Picasso's observation about artists: *Every child is an artist. The problem is how to remain an artist once he grows up.* As the infant matures, it is totally enveloped by the veil of illusion, until everything is witnessed through that veil. Thus, the world becomes almost entirely populated by unenlightened individuals all living the same shared illusion. Obviously, the newborn is helpless and needs nurturing as it grows; it needs to develop emotionally, psychologically and kinaesthetically to give it the best chance of surviving and functioning effectively in the world. However, this comes at a price: it loses what it came into the world with; it loses what could be called the original state.

Occasionally, despite a lifetime of conditioning, a small number of adults inexplicably awaken to their true nature, returning them to this original state – *the I before I am*. Sometimes without volition and sometimes through an apparent cultivation, the veil drops. One or two of this select group may talk or write about how they now experience life, and seekers revere them as enlightened beings. To add to the drama, some *Enlightened Ones* appear to encourage a seeker/guru relationship, perhaps in an attempt to communicate within the illusion – *a thorn to remove a thorn, so to speak*, which generates more followers, and the Sage is born. In fact, there is a long lineage of students turned gurus, each dedicating their Enlightenment to their master. However, no one has become anything; all that has happened is the unenlightened state has fallen away, revealing the indescribable being-ness of the newborn child, experienced and interpreted (*with mixed results*) through a conditioned adult mind.

The phenomenon of Enlightenment and the enlightened guru are illusions in the sense that they can only exist within the world of separation, but these illusions seem to have a greater significance because of the gravitas given to them by obsequious devotees blinded by their desire for Liberation. Spiritual seekers embarking upon these journeys are spinning an additional web to add to their already complex life stories. The important thing to them is that they see a gradual progression, and are able to regularly reflect upon their spiritual advances. They want to feel they are achieving increasing levels of self-awareness, leading to peaceful thoughts and right action. Their resolve will hold strong so long as they believe such progress is being made.

Their goals may be Liberation and Enlightenment, but as they work towards emptying the mind and purifying the heart, believing they are closing in on a personal transformation, they are unwittingly achieving the exact opposite. Any apparent success will have a familiar hollow feel, because it is built upon an illusion. Those things the Self struggles to control – capriciousness, randomness, change and uncertainty – are the very things that point to its inherent emptiness, and so it continually wrestles with them in an attempt to impose order and maintain its own pretence. Pursuing Enlightenment is simply another attempt to give substance to something that does not exist; it is the ultimate adornment for the Self.

Away from the popular illusion of Enlightenment, and the complex self-delusional games played by those attempting to achieve it, are rare individuals for whom the process of becoming 'unenlightened' never quite worked, in other words by a bizarre quirk of fate, their conditioning failed to create a believable Self. For them, the veil of illusion is threadbare, and glimpses of the Absolute regularly confirm their true nature – though not in ways the intellect can capture or express. Their life is a paradox: its seriousness is also its absurdity, and they find playing the game both ridiculous and sublime. They have a foot in both worlds but belong to neither. Life is beautiful and confusing, simple and complex, intelligent and insane, and simultaneously experienced as both a roller coaster of highs and lows, and as a single constant event. They are at the same time disconnected from the experience and at its very core – a perpetual twilight existence where darkness and light meet, and both are negated leaving something indescribable. They appear as entrenched in the illusion as the next person, seemingly buying into the story of 'me', but at the same time are in touch with a deeper awareness. Living a kind of incongruous existence, they follow the life-games people play without really believing in them. Occasionally their mask slips and at times their behaviour can appear quite comical, and at other times, quite mad. They may be pitied because they appear out of step with the rest of the world.

Those living this twilight existence are perfectly aware they are perceived as different, but they have no desire to change, nor could they if they wanted. Such individuals are simply glimpsing things as they are, free from the constraints of a shared conditioning. You may relate to this – I can, as it is drawn from my own experience. I lived like this for most of my life, seeing the light but living in the dark. Occasionally the veil of illusion lifted but fear of letting go and losing my Self kept me imprisoned. I chose the world of forms despite knowing deep down they were untrue; until at some point the 'I' that apparently chose disappeared, and that 'deep down' place became home.

Lost in a moment without a Self, what remains cannot be named, described or comprehended, and does not need to name, describe or comprehend. When that moment is over and you reappear, leave that experience well alone and it will return from time to time, but never when you want – only occasionally when you are not there. The Absolute is silent and still – emptiness neither containing nor contained, a sense of the moment outside of time, solid and ephemeral. Behind everything it is there, indescribable and obvious – a brightness that blinds.

19

SETTING SAIL

The Absolute comes before existence and brings forth existence and
is being and non-being.
It is the outpouring of everything that has been, that is and ever
will be.
It is the infinite, outside of time and space, and the ticking
clock as each second passes.
It is a speck of dust suspended in sunlight and the
myriad of swirling galaxies in the mind's eye.
It is the emptiness that gives rise to all and
the fullness contained therein.
It is impersonal and negates the Self.
It cannot be named or known.
It is ubiquitous but unseen.
It is veiled by illusion
and it is the illusion.
It is not me nor
you.
It is one, not
two.
It is the I
before
I am

•

COLIN McMORRAN

SETTING SAIL

The intention of this book is not to create more concepts, but to question the concepts we already have – specifically the concept of the Self, an idea that most people never address. To use a sailing analogy: if the questioning has been successful, your vessel has been untethered from its moorings and set adrift. Floating away from the safety of the harbour as the tide pulls you into the enormity of the ocean. However, this is what your vessel was built for; sailing the ocean is its function. You are leaving behind those who believe they need the protection of the harbour; for them, as long as they are securely moored to the dock, comfort is found in the gentle ebb and flow of the tide. For some, even the movement of the tide is disconcerting and so they keep their vessel in dry-dock where it is completely disassociated from its function and where there is no movement or connection to the ocean.

There are different levels of conscious awareness: many people are completely detached from the movement of the ocean, unable to see beyond their personal stories and the chatter in the head, living solely within that myopic and fixed paradigm they are in dry-dock. Some are moored to the dock feeling the underlying ebb and flow of the tide, vaguely sensing a deeper level of consciousness within their everyday lives. Others are sailing within the safety of the harbour walls getting a feel for the sea and exploring a deeper awareness. Those who have awakened to pure consciousness have left the harbour behind and are sailing the ocean. This analogy may give the impression there are progressive stages of consciousness; however, awakening can happen in an instant or conversely the same level of consciousness can last a lifetime. So, someone in dry-dock can suddenly find themselves pitched into the ocean, which can be extremely disconcerting and it can take years to find their sea legs. For those who have spent time exploring within the harbour walls entering the ocean may be less bewildering. Alternatively, someone can spend their entire life moored to the dockside, their only connection with the ocean being the gentle ebb and flow of the tide.

Any movement in consciousness, whether from dry-dock to dockside, or harbour to ocean, is moving from the known to the unknown and can be daunting. The natural inclination is to stay with the safety of the known. However, as the ocean beckons, you will begin to realise the vessel is at home there, and start to sense its affinity with the sea as it rises and falls effortlessly with the swells. The movement you experience as the vessel cuts through the water gives a sense of freedom you have never experienced and with the wind in your face and the sea air filling your senses you feel more truly alive than ever before. Allowing the vessel to be what it was meant to be and fulfil its natural function is liberating, and you will smile as you realise worries about your ability to sail were totally unfounded – this is what you were born for. Feeling at one with both vessel and ocean, you realise the safety of the harbour was a prison you created for yourself, and for the first time in your life you taste real freedom.

For us to set sail into the deeper consciousness of *the I before I am* we must first realise the prison we have made for ourselves. This 'prison of our minds' has been discussed throughout this book: it is the personal story we carry with us that limits and defines who we believe we are. It forces us to live in the past or project into the future and therefore misses the present moment. It tells us that we have limited time and must make a success of our lives by achieving certain material (and spiritual) goals. It tells us we are limited individuals who have to prove ourselves by measuring up to other people's expectations, and must strive to reach our full potential (I should point out that as manifestations of the Absolute we have unlimited potential, however the way most of us 'strive' to achieve it is counterproductive as we fixate on the external world before understanding our inner truth). The prison of our mind tells us that happiness is found in the world of forms and so we become a measure of our possessions and achievements, and it tells us that we are in lack and the only way to become whole is through other people's validation or by finding that special person to complete us.

I transcend this is a direct way of questioning that story by loosening the ropes that bind us to it – the tide will do the rest. Continuing to practice *I transcend this* from within the illusion is like tentatively exploring within the harbour walls. Sailing into the ocean, however, cannot be a conscious decision, it will happen when it happens; just as when learning to ride a bicycle, you can never plan for that split second rush when you find yourself pedalling unassisted for the first time.

As your connection with the ocean grows, it becomes clear that the story of the illusionary Self you have been clinging to your whole life was a prison, initially created through your conditioning and then perpetuated by repetition and normalised through mutual agreement. Once the Self took root, it became an almost impenetrable fortress, guarded night and day by the ego. Living in the eternal present and being in touch with *the I before I am*, you will meet life with an open heart rather than a closed mind. Every person and every experience entering your life will be accepted and embraced at face value, rather than judged by a fixed personality with its story of how people should act or how events should unfold. Freedom is liberation from your vice-like mind and a return to the open expanse of the oceanic freedom where once again you are one with the natural flow of life.

Your 'vessel' (*of course it is not 'yours'*) is the body-mind with all its conditioning and cumulative experiences. If it has been conditioned to sit in dry-dock then it knows nothing else – its fixed mind-set divides everything into constituent parts, and dissects and categorises in an attempt to conceptualise, understand and then control. This is most people's reality; they may have a vague idea of the ocean but will question or deny its existence because they can see no evidence of it in their lives. They have been raised and educated by others, all of whom are in dry-dock, and therefore those who talk of sailing the ocean are met with scepticism or ridicule. They look for safety in knowledge and understanding in an effort to minimise change and tame the unknown, and they suffer because of it. You are designed to sail the ocean not stagnate on the dockside, and there is a deep primordial awareness of this. All it takes is a willingness to open one's mind to other possibilities. While the dockside seems a safe place it actually creates immense suffering because of the constant need to control life and the expectations of how it should unfold and so you fight a continual battle against what is.

Recognition of the ocean's reality can happen after years of personal suffering or through contact with those who experience it directly, or a combination of both. Recognition is the opening, once the body-mind realises it is immersed in the ocean and at one with the great source then the egoic mind, while continuing to perform a pragmatic function, is no longer the captain – it becomes the second-mate. You are no longer the constrained entity at the mercy of your conditioning but rather an open expanse of possibilities. The egoic mind is usurped and works in the service of the Absolute. You come alive in the ocean, never to return to the safety of the harbour, finding peace being what you truly are: divine presence arising from the one source. This book is an attempt to untie the ropes that bind you, ending your repetitive thought patterns and liberating you from the illusion of a Self. Once you are set free upon the ocean the worn pathways of your thoughts are washed away and every present moment is born afresh.

20
CURTAIN CALL

*One moon shows in every pool; in every pool,
the one moon.*

ZEN PROVERB

*That you carry yourself forward and experience the myriad things is delusion.
That the myriad things come forward and experience themselves is awakening*

DOGEN ZENJI

The Absolute originates neither in the heart nor the head, but expresses through both,
Has no need for intellect, insight or intuition, but speaks through them all,
Does not require goals, gods or gurus, but embraces each,
Has no need for faith, fear or fortitude, but accepts them all,
Cannot falter, fail or falsify and neither triumphs nor asserts the truth.
Animating everything, it attaches to nothing,
Being and non-being – the emptiness that births all,
Knowing nothing, for there is nothing it needs to know,
Its strength is immeasurable, yet its touch gentle as the breeze,
Greater than all, it is less than nothing,
Knowing not its splendour, it illuminates the world,
Existing in the present – eternity is its home,
Un-nameable and unknowable, even to itself,
Unaware it is God, it transcends all.

COLIN McMORRAN

We cannot control or make sense of our life through concepts, ideas or beliefs. Instead, recognise that the desire to do so comes from an illusion, and if you ask what will you do without belief in your Self, how can you survive, what will happen if the illusionary Self falls away and 'you' disappear then know it is the egoic mind clinging to these questions like someone drowning clings to a life raft. Whenever there is the faintest possibility of freedom from the Self these fears about a future without a story arise. Freedom is frightening because the Self believes it will lose control and autonomy, when in fact freedom is the realisation that it does not have control or autonomy. The person clinging to their life raft is dreaming – in reality they are actually safe in bed clinging to pillows, upon awakening there will be a huge sense of relief mixed with amusement. Just as in the nightmare, there is often a faint sense that it is unreal, so too in the daily dream of life a deeper truth is often sensed.

Each time you wonder whether you are acting from pure awareness, each time you praise yourself for staying present, each time you are pleased to have controlled your undesirable emotions – you are back in the illusion. Each time you take credit for right thought or right action – you are back in the illusion. So watch for these traps; do not replace an unconscious illusionary Self with a spiritually aware, but conceited, one. Be vigilant and unyielding; every time a self-conscious thought arises, repeat *I transcend this*.

Take what you need from the teachings of others but do not mistake the master for their words; we cannot walk in another's footsteps and attempting to do so is the greatest folly. Rather than chasing Enlightenment or Liberation – understand instead that they are part of the illusion. Focus upon the illusion itself: be aware of how you breathe life into your egoic mind and perpetuate your story; direct attention to the illusionary Self and notice how it lives predominantly in either the past or the future. Notice how it skips the present moment; almost as if afraid to be there, perhaps sensing it cannot survive in pure presence. Do not search for your true Self, just observe the false Self – that is all.

❈

As this play of words draws to a close and the time to leave the theatre approaches, we – *the audience* – may recognise that pang of loss felt at the end of a performance. As we sit in silence, the empty stage forms a rectangular oasis of light within the dark theatre and our thoughts turn to daily life and our return to the 'real' world.

While contemplating any effect this book may have had upon us and questioning what – *if anything* – we have learnt, our attention is drawn back to the stage, as a spotlight picks up a lone figure emerging from the wings. The light follows as the figure crosses to the front of the stage and stands in the footlights head bowed. Fidgeting nervously, we feel an inexpressible familiarity with the character and wonder who the performer is. We become aware of the audience's quiet murmurings building to a steady drone that reverberates around the theatre.

The figure begins a slow handclap, gradually silencing the audience as our attention is focused upon each successive clap ringing out crisp and clear in the moment. After what seems an eternity, the figure abruptly stops, and in the deafening silence that follows time stands still. The enigmatic figure looks up surveying the entire audience and making brief eye contact with each of us, and with an almost imperceptible smile and an outstretched sweep of the arm takes a bow. We, the audience, reciprocate – hypnotically bowing our heads and closing our eyes in unison.

CURTAIN CALL

With your eyes closed and head bowed, you enter a timeless state where thoughts cannot touch you and where there is no striving, you feel identity falling away, but this time you do not fight it. Unaware of the passage of time you eventually, and with some trepidation, open your eyes. You are now seeing from a different perspective: you are standing on stage squinting into the lights – *you are that dark figure*. Disorientated and with your eyes adjusting to the brightness, you look around the theatre and see that all the seats are empty, there is no audience – *there never was*. Your stomach rolls at the realisation you are both performer and audience in your own play. Your story and its central character is just an illusion played to an imaginary audience in your mind to create and maintain the idea of 'you'. It is realised that sustaining and serving that illusionary Self is not only exhausting but that belief in your story and breathing life into it brings untold suffering. You realise there was only ever 'one' and that separation was an illusion.

Now, standing in the spotlight, with the play between performer and audience over, there is enormous relief in letting go and stepping outside of your story. The spotlight and the footlights die, pitching the theatre into darkness and with no background forms, no characters and no story, you merge back into the eternal as the fabricated confines of the theatre and the claustrophobic life you have been living disappear. Light fills your heart and love pours from you as the illusion of your Self dissolves into pure conscious awareness, returning you to the source prior to personification – *the I before I am*. The show's over and the curtain falls on the illusionary Self.

APPENDIX

Analogies, metaphors and parables working from within the illusion of a separate Self can tap into the eternal source and echo back the truth of our being. It is quite remarkable when an illusionary play of words resonates at this deeper level, but it will be difficult to understand and articulate such a feeling, so try not to grasp at meaning and instead allow the words to wash over you and perhaps the underlying truth of your being will gradually seep into your conscious awareness.

All of the great spiritual teachings work through analogy and metaphor, it is only when scripture is taken literally that religious dogma and prejudice arise. Good analogies serve as pointers to the truth because they come from a position grounded within the illusion and can cast light upon an otherwise esoteric subject by focusing instead upon something familiar that fits your worldview. Where analogies are concerned I have found a scattergun approach has a better chance of hitting the target than a single shot and hope at least one resonates with you at this deeper level. Of course, the effectiveness of the message depends upon the readiness of the receiver; nevertheless, at the right time and in the right conditions, a spark from the known can jump the void and ignite the unknown.

THE OCEAN WAVE

Waves are a manifestation of the ocean, arising as the seabed slows the incoming tide causing the surface flow to swell up and overturn. Although the familiar sight and sound of crashing white foam appears separate and identifiable, it is always part of the ocean, and never separates from it. It makes no sense to imagine a wave independent from the ocean: the two are one and the same. Similarly, we are temporary manifestations of the Absolute, apparently being born, having our moment and then returning to the source. Just as each wave has a unique form as it swells and breaks, so too our environment uniquely shapes us as we grow. And just as the wave is created and sustained through constant movement, so our life is created and sustained through continual change.

Waves are tangible and physically exist; we can distinguish between them and can measure their progress and witness their different forms. However, we know their appearance, their motion and force are manifestations of the one underlying source. Their separateness is both real and unreal; we know that although each individual wave is unique and there will never be two the same, they do not act autonomously and cannot exist independently from the ocean. Similarly, our separateness is both real and unreal; we do not act autonomously and have no existence independent from the Absolute. We are unique expressions of the one underlying source.

THE SNAKE

Walking in the woods towards the end of the day in fading light, you come across a snake on the path ahead. Gripped with fear, you are frozen to the spot. Your heart races as you anxiously wait for it to continue into the undergrowth, but it remains stationary. Sensing that something's amiss, you tentatively take a step closer, and with great relief, realise it is a length of rope! Your experience has been transformed, and you continue on your way stepping over the rope with a smile. During the experience, nothing externally changed: the rope was always a rope and nothing more, but due to ignorance caused by a misperception, you saw a snake. This caused psychological reactions, including fear and anxiety, and physiological responses, such as an increased heart rate and tense muscles. In that moment, the illusionary snake and all the associated physical and emotional responses were your reality. Then upon further enquiry, that reality changed and relief replaced the fear. Stepping over the rope, you smiled to yourself over the needless stress it caused.

You live life believing you are an individual with all the stresses, fears and psychological suffering that entails. Then one day the reality of your situation becomes apparent: you realise what you thought was real is an illusion and that your suffering was caused by a misperception. What previously caused you stress and anxiety is now seen as unreal and when you are faced with life's apparent dangers you will smile, but not to your Self, for that will be long gone.

THE MOVIE

Movies are a popular escape from everyday life. For a few hours we allow ourselves to enter into another world populated by fictional characters living fictional lives. We voyeuristically lose ourselves in the dancing images as the characters play out their roles and the story unfolds. Although we realise it is created specifically to entertain us and we are complicit in the whole charade, we nevertheless hope to connect with the main characters and experience a roller coaster of emotions through them. Throughout the movie, we feel safe in the knowledge that whatever emotions arise within us, no matter how perilous, frightening or upsetting, we cannot be harmed. We know it is a dance of light and sound, but in the name of entertainment, we consciously buy into the illusion of the moving images. Regardless of our strong emotional responses, we realise there is a fundamental difference between the character's lives and our own; it is obvious that our on-screen heroes have no ability to change the direction of the movie; it is a *fait accompli*, burned in celluloid (or digitally captured) months or even years before. This is so obvious it hardly needs stating – everyone watching knows, nevertheless, we allow ourselves to be drawn into the characters plight, feeling for them and living through their experiences in real time. Your destiny is as fixed as those on-screen characters, and just as the movie has a running time, so your life appears to have duration.

THE OPTICAL ILLUSION

You may be familiar with the optical illusion consisting of two heads in white silhouette facing each other over a black background. Viewed one way it appears to be two faces looking at each other, but viewed differently, it appears as a sculptured black vase on a white background. What you see depends upon how you choose to view it. If you see two faces, then by focusing attention upon the space between, the picture flips and the black vase appears. We are programmed to contrast and filter, and then select and compare in a constant effort to recognise and name, by doing so we make sense of the world and can function within it; for example, when viewing abstract art a representation of something familiar is sought in an attempt to extract meaning.

This vase illusion is a very simple example of this selective processing: through concentration, the picture can be flipped between two completely different images with different meanings and associations. There are many illusions of this kind, some more elaborate than others, but what they all have in common is the fascinating property of appearing to be two (or several) distinctly different things without any change in the underlying forms. The vase and the faces are subjectively flipped in and out of existence, but the underlying contrasting black and white shapes remain unchanged and unaffected All that changes is the subjective meaning in the mind of the perceiver.

Underlying all apparent forms is an impersonal emptiness holding everything and giving birth to all manifestations; the underlying black and white shapes prior to being objectified through subjective perception are analogous to the changeless underlying reality – *the I before I am*. It is as difficult for us to see through the illusionary Self and witness our true nature as it is for us to see the underlying black and white shapes without turning them into objects like faces or vases. When this underlying changeless nothing is perceived (subjectively witnessed) it becomes *every-thing*: trees, humans, planets, gods, waves, bowls, viruses, analogies, thoughts and actions. We are constantly creating forms from the one underlying Absolute.

THE BOWL

Our body-minds can be likened to a bowl: the emptiness of the bowl gives its function, the bowl is utilised by filling that emptiness. We believe that to function we need to fill our bowl with the experiences of life, and then we define ourselves by its contents. However, we are neither the bowl nor its contents – we are the emptiness that allows the bowl to fill. We are the emptiness that comes before everything, giving rise to all manifestations – the Absolute that contains all multiplicities. *We shape clay into a pot, but it is the emptiness inside that holds whatever we want. We work with being, but non-being is what we use* (Tao Te Ching)

BIBLIOGRAPHY

Augustine, St. (2016) *The Confessions of St. Augustine – Translator Joseph Green Pilkington* North Charleston SC: Createspace.

Author unknown (1905) *The Kena Upanishad with Shankara's Commentary. Translated by Sitarama Sastri. S.* [Online] Available at: https://www.universaltheosophy.com/pdf-library/upanishads/Volume%201%20-%20Isa,%20Kena%20&%20Mundaka%20Upanishads.pdf.

Balsekar, R. (1992) *Consciousness Speaks* California: Advaita Press.

Bohr, N. (1987) *The Philosophical Writings of Niels Bohr.* Woodbridge, CT: Oxbow Press.

Börne, L. (2012) *Volumes 6–7, Collected Writings.* Berlin: Nabu Press.

Camus, A. (1942) *The Outsider or The Stranger (L'Étranger).* London: Penguin Modern Classics.

Da Vinci, L. (2008) *Notebooks.* London: Oxford University Press.

Descartes (2010) *R. Meditations – Translated by Desmond M. Clarke.* London: Penguin Books.

Dewey, J. (2008) *Democracy and Education Radford.* VA: Wilder Publications.

Diderot, D. (1762) *Rameanu's Nephew.* [Online] Available at: https://books.google.co.uk/books/about/Le_Neveu_de_Rameau.

html?id=hL1pDAAAQBAJ&printsec=frontcover&source=kp_read_button&redir_esc=y#v=onepage&q&f=false.

Einstein, A. (2006) *The World As I See*. New York: Citadel Press.

Eliot, T. S. (2001) *Four Quartets*. London: Faber & Faber.

Emerson, R. W. (2015) *Ralph Waldo Emerson – Delphi Poets Series*. Hastings: Delphi Publishing.

Hafele, J. C. & Keating, E. Around-the-World Atomic Clocks: Predicted Relativistic Time Gains – Science, New Series, Vol. 177, No. 4044 (Jul. 14, 1972), 166-168. American Association for the Advancement of Science.

Jordan, P. (1974) *The Philosophy of Quantum Mechanics by Max Jammer*. New Jersey: Wiley-Blackwell.

Judge, W. Q. (1965) *Bhagavad-Gita: The Book of Devotion, from the Sanskrit*. Bombay: Theosophy Company (India).

Maharaj, N. (2012) *I Am That: Talks with Sri Nisargadatta Maharaj –Translated by Maurice Frydman*. London: Acorn Press.

Osho. (2011) *Living Dangerously – Ordinary Enlightenment for Extraordinary Times*. London: Watkins Publishing .

Parsons, T. (2005) *It is Seen, but there's no-one seeing It*. (Han van den Boogaard speaking with Tony Parsons Amsterdam). [Online] http://hanvandenboogaard.nl/interviews/interview-han-met-tony-parsons.

Planck, M. (1936) *The philosophy of physics*. London: W. W. Norton & Company.

Pope, A. (2002) *Miscellanies in Prose and Verse by Poe, Swift and Gay, Vol. 4*. Oxford: Routledge.

Porchia, A. (2003) *Voices (Voces) English translation by W. S. Merwin*. Washington: Copper Canyon Press.

Rumi J. (1995) *Selected Poems Translated by Coleman Banks*. London: Penguin Books.

Sankara, A (Shankaracharya, Shankara) (2012) *Powerful Quotes From Sankara*. The Freedom Religion Press.

Schrodinger, E. (2009) *My View of The World* – translated by Cecily Hastings. London: Cambridge University Press.

Schrodinger, E. (1931) *The Observer*. London: Observer Newspaper.

Seng-chao. (1968) *Chao Lun, the treatises of Seng-Chao* – translated by Walter Liebenthal. Hong Kong: Hong Kong University Press.

Suzuki, D. T. (1994) *An Introduction to Zen Buddhism*. New York: Grove Press.

Suzuki, S. (2011) *Zen Mind, Beginner's Mind*. Boston: Shambhala.

Sweeney, J. M. (2013) *Francis of Assisi in His Own Words: The Essential Writings*. Brewster, MA: Paraclete Press.

Tolle, E. *The Role of Vigilance in Transforming Consciousness* [Online] Available at: https://www.facebook.com/Eckharttolle/videos/eckhart-tolle-tv-vigilance/10151519352410831/.

Tzu, L. (2015) *Tao Te Ching* – translated by Stephen Mitchell. London: Frances Lincoln.

Voltaire (1977) *The Portable Voltaire, Edited by Ben Ray Redman*. England: Penguin.

Wilde, O. (1894) *A Few Maxims For The Instruction Of The Over-Educated*. [Online] Available at: https://en.wikisource.org/wiki/A_Few_Maxims_For_The_Instruction_Of_The_Over-Educated.

Young, T. (1802) *The Bakerian lecture On the theory of light and colours*. London: W.Bulmer.

Zander, B. (2000) *The Art of Possibility*. Harvard Business School Press.

Zenji, D. (2000) *Enlightenment Unfolds: The Essential Teachings of Zen Master Dogen*. Colorado: Shambhala Publications.

seeingnow.com

Made in United States
Troutdale, OR
05/04/2025